## DID YOU KNOW . . .

. . . that John Wilkes Booth may have had the backing of an international cabal in his assassination of Abraham Lincoln, including Vice President Andrew Johnson?

. . . the long-dreaded and much-foreboded government specter known as Big Brother is not only a figment of our imagined future, but a very real and powerful entity that is already in existence?

. . . that the legendary "black helicopters" that the government uses on its covert domestic operations pursued and threatened the residents of a small Louisiana town for over a week with absolutely no actions being taken by the lawful authorities?

. . . that the often joked-about difference between packages holding ten hot dogs and packages holding eight hot dog buns is, in reality, one of the biggest consumer frauds in history?

. . . that your own doctor may be part of a conspiracy that involves aliens, the deliberate manufacturing of sickness and disease, and the sinister plot to fleece billions of dollars from the public in the search for a "cure"—which is being withheld *on* 

**WELL, NOW**
**CO**

# Conspiracy Theories

*Edited by*
**Kate Tuckett**

**BERKLEY BOOKS, NEW YORK**

**THE BERKLEY PUBLISHING GROUP**
**Published by the Penguin Group**
**Penguin Group (USA) Inc.**
**375 Hudson Street, New York, New York 10014, USA**
Penguin Group (Canada), 90 Eglinton Avenue East, Suite 700, Toronto, Ontario M4P 2Y3, Canada
(a division of Pearson Penguin Canada Inc.)
Penguin Books Ltd., 80 Strand, London WC2R 0RL, England
Penguin Group Ireland, 25 St. Stephen's Green, Dublin 2, Ireland (a division of Penguin Books Ltd.)
Penguin Group (Australia), 250 Camberwell Road, Camberwell, Victoria 3124, Australia
(a division of Pearson Australia Group Pty. Ltd.)
Penguin Books India Pvt. Ltd., 11 Community Centre, Panchsheel Park, New Delhi—110 017, India
Penguin Group (NZ), Cnr. Airborne and Rosedale Roads, Albany, Auckland 1310, New Zealand
(a division of Pearson New Zealand Ltd.)
Penguin Books (South Africa) (Pty.) Ltd., 24 Sturdee Avenue, Rosebank, Johannesburg 2196,
South Africa

Penguin Books Ltd., Registered Offices: 80 Strand, London WC2R 0RL, England

CONSPIRACY THEORIES

A Berkley Book / published by arrangement with Summersdale Publishers Ltd.

PRINTING HISTORY
Previously published in Great Britain by Summersdale Publishers Ltd., 2004
Berkley mass-market edition / September 2005

ISBN: 0-425-20527-4

BERKLEY®
Berkley Books are published by The Berkley Publishing Group,
a division of Penguin Group (USA) Inc.,
375 Hudson Street, New York, New York 10014.
BERKLEY is a registered trademark of Penguin Group (USA) Inc.
The "B" design is a trademark belonging to Penguin Group (USA) Inc.

PRINTED IN THE UNITED STATES OF AMERICA

10  9  8  7  6  5  4  3  2  1

# Contents

# Introduction

The archetypal conspiracy theory might go something like this: There is a clandestine secret society in our midst. . . . They are alien to all we believe in and are about to seize control of the world. . . . They are everywhere. . . . They are ruthless and powerful. . . . They are sexually corrupt. . . . They perform the most heinous crimes known to mankind.

Belief in conspiracy theories is more than just the belief in an occasional underhand plot. It is a belief system that asserts that world events are being governed in secret by a group of ultrapowerful puppeteers behind the scenes. While little may be done about this sorry state of affairs, at least we can have the satisfaction of having worked out what is going on.

Of course, one can argue that obsession with conspiracy theories serves only to demonstrate the lunatic paranoia running rife in the twentieth and twenty-first centuries. Much talk about conspiracies is dismissed as paranoia and much of it is paranoia. But in reality, history has proved all too well that politicians lie, presidents lie and bureaucrats lie. If we continue to be gullible and believe everything that is presented to us, the truth will never come out. It becomes not only interesting and revealing but an absolute priority to question authority and, more specifically, the authoritarians.

Why is it that we can accept that Tony Blair's smile is as broad as it appears? Or that the American CIA assassinated the president of Chile, but we cannot believe that they would assassinate their own? Why is it that we can accept that governments would experiment on their citizens with plutonium, syphilis and nerve gas, but don't consider that they would use the AIDS virus? Why did the German populace accept in the first place that Hitler was trustworthy?

Conspiracy theories are not new. It is believed that Nero concocted an elaborate tale to shift the blame to the Christians for the burning of Rome. Hitler was a master of such deceit. And, undoubtedly, when conspiracies fail to accurately predict world events, this only serves to prove their credibility. Double bluff is refined to an art form.

It cannot be denied that controversy has often accompanied many of the pivotal turning points of Western civilization. Many major events, for better or for worse, have occurred as the result of people behind the scenes who have held the keys to the actions of the world. Startling discoveries, often stretching far back into history, can affect the very way our Western thought processes and behavior patterns are conducted. And that is not to mention such terrifying revelations as the Elvis Killed Kennedy conspiracy or the real reason for Santa's oversized hat. Read on. . . .

# 9/11

The "War on Terror" is said to have begun on September 11, 2001. But is it possible that the war began before this date? Some people point to U.S. government complicity in the events of 9/11, either by not doing enough to prevent it, or—more ominously—by actively planning for it. Whatever the truth may be, there is plenty of conjecture that what happened on that day doesn't add up to the popular version of the events.

What is not in dispute is that public support for the War on Terror was far greater after these attacks than it would have been on September 10, 2001. Could it be that the attacks were allowed to happen to create public clamor for a war that would otherwise have been inconceivable? Many people have pointed to the possibility that 9/11 was a clone of Pearl Harbor, an attack on the U.S. that was deliberately allowed to take place in order to further the war aims of a president. But a more sinister comparison has been made by those skeptical of the motives of the Bush administration. They claim that what happened was more akin to Adolf Hitler's burning of the Reichstag, the German Republic's parliament, on February 27, 1933. Hitler blamed the fire on

Communists plotting against the state. But historians widely accept the view that a member of the Prussian interior ministry set fire to the building deliberately, on Hitler's orders. Immediately after the fire Hitler announced an emergency decree which suspended the normal civilian rights and liberties of citizens and gave the government enormous authority to impose order. This was the beginning of the end for democratic values and the rise of Nazi dictatorship.

On October 3, 2001 Congress approved Bush's Patriot Act, a similar bill which reduced the civil liberties of Americans and allowed the detention without trial of anyone the government deemed a potential "security threat." Furthermore, the public and political pressure for retaliation for the attacks was intense, and neatly tied into the agenda of the "Project for a New American Century." This was a strategic document put forward by a group of neoconservatives in September 2000 outlining a new strategy for American global dominance in the twenty-first century. This think tank included Dick Cheney, the vice president; Donald Rumsfeld, secretary of defense; Paul Wolfowitz, his deputy; Jeb Bush, brother of George and governor of Florida; and Lewis Libby, the leader of Bush's 2000 election campaign team now working in the White House.

The most intriguing part of the document concerns the readjustment of American forces across the globe. The report states that only an incremental approach can be taken to this radical restructuring owing to political and public constraints, unless there was "some catastrophic and catalyzing event like a new Pearl Harbor."

Despite all this, however, there is still the question of how such an elaborate attack could have been prepared and executed by the government and its agencies without the media becoming deeply suspicious. The most likely explanation is that the attacks were planned by Osama bin Laden and Al Qaeda but that U.S. intelligence agencies did not act upon the information they received to adequately prevent them. Evidence of their failure, whether deliberate or through incompetence, has been widespread following Congressional investigations but without any smoking gun. Furthermore, the CIA and New York City counterterrorism offices were based in Building 7 of the World Trade Center and were therefore destroyed, along with any potentially incriminating evidence.

The suspicions about intelligence are just part of the growing mistrust about the events that day, which reverberated right around the world. On the day of the attacks geological surveys in New York recorded the greatest amount of seismic activity as occurring immediately before the Twin Towers collapsed, and not when they hit the ground. This has led many people to the conclusion that the towers were blown up with explosives underneath the building and not by the enormous volume of fuel that ignited after the two airliners exploded; a belief reinforced by the way the towers imploded inwards instead of collapsing sideways.

The evidence at the Pentagon also raises profound questions. Why was the Pentagon hit on the one side of the building that happened to be empty on the day of the attacks owing to refurbishment? Why was there no visible evidence of a destroyed airliner among the debris? Why were no fighter jets scrambled to intercept the hijacked aircraft until after the third plane had hit the Pentagon, despite it being a legal requirement in the U.S. for fighter jets to be scrambled whenever a commercial airliner veers significantly off its flight path? How was so much information known about the hijackers and released to the media by the FBI so soon after the attacks, including details on a passport miraculously found among the rubble of the Twin Towers?

These question marks raise serious doubts about the official version of what happened on September 11. Many are cynical of the report published only a year prior to that date; a report which would revolutionize America's role in the world toward ultimate military, political and social hegemony, but one which would require a catastrophic event. These cynics cannot accept that the occurrence of just such an event can be no more than coincidence. Can it also be mere coincidence that those who authored the report are responsible for failing to prevent the attack and for coordinating their desired global response?

# Abraham Lincoln

Abraham Lincoln was shot by John Wilkes Booth on April 14, 1865. And questions surrounding the assassination arose immediately. Was Booth solely responsible for the assassination? Or was he simply a tool in a much larger conspiracy?

The vice president's role in the whole mystery is unclear to say the least. About seven hours before the assassination of the president, Booth stopped at the Washington hotel, residence of Andrew Johnson, the vice president. Learning that neither Johnson nor his private secretary were present, Booth wrote the following note: "Don't wish to disturb you. Are you at home? J. Wilkes Booth." Johnson's private secretary testified to the fact that he found the note later in the afternoon. So from this can we assume that Johnson and Booth knew each other?

Many people thought that Johnson was involved with the assassination, and a special Assassination Committee was established to investigate any evidence linking him to Lincoln's death. Nothing suspicious was ever found by the committee, yet a belief that he was in some way involved continued for many years. It certainly seems suspicious that Booth should have sought him out so shortly before the assassination.

Of course, rather than having been controlled by someone else, Booth himself could have been in control of a number of coconspirators who were then either hanged or imprisoned at Ft. Jefferson. Booth could have been defending Southern values of slavery and racism. The assassination could have been a rather more dramatic solution than was initially intended. Booth may have intended merely to kidnap the president and to demand prisoners of war in return. The assassination could have been a simple step further when the kidnapping plans fell through.

It would appear, according to a series of letters found in Booth's possession, that he knew of a plot to blow up the White House. Certainly if this was the case, if the plot had disintegrated, more daring and radical planning would have been necessary in order to carry out the original objectives of the conspirators. In this sense, perhaps the original plot was far smaller in scale and the whole thing was a reckless afterthought when original plans went wrong.

Lincoln had made himself a considerable number of enemies as a result of his financial policies. His Civil War efforts had eaten into his financial resources but he had declined high-interest offers of loans from European bankers led by the Rothschilds and had found other ways to fund the war. More importantly, the British bankers opposed Lincoln's protectionist policies. Some Englishmen in the 1860s believed that "British free trade, industrial monopoly and human slavery travel together." Lincoln was thus viewed as a threat to the established order of things and was possibly assassinated as a result.

# AIDS

AIDS is quite possibly one of the most horrific developments this past century. Millions of dollars are being poured into research and yet a cure still seems all but completely elusive. Gone are the days of carefree sex 'n' drugs 'n' rock 'n' roll, as the deadly virus does not seem to be at all choosy in who it targets.

Shocking as the whole phenomenon would be if this really was a natural plague, theory has it that the AIDS virus was in fact artificially manufactured by the U.S. government to kill African-Americans and this is being taken very seriously by the black community. Rumors are being circulated that the disease was developed to kill off the so-called "useless eaters" of the human race—blacks, homosexuals and drug users to be more precise. The Minister of Health for Louis Farrakhan's Nation of Islam, Dr. Abdul Alim Muhammed, has called for a formal investigation. In his words:

"We know from the Congressional Report that money was appropriated for the creation of artificial biological agents to defeat the human immune system. This took place in July of 1969. Ten million dollars was allocated to the U.S. army. So . . . let there be hearings to uncover the files."

Many African-Americans quote this experiment, which took place at Tuskegee as grounds for skepticism about the government's intentions. From 1932 to 1972 about four hundred poor black men were used as guinea pigs as scientists studied the effects of syphilis left untreated. And what's more, as Thomas Blocker, Director of Health Professions at Morehouse College says: "A number of people have the idea that there's always the possibility that people who are disadvantaged may be used as guinea pigs in terms of medicine."

We cannot know about the origins of AIDS. We do not know whether the most lethal worldwide killer was born of some warped conspiracy in the name of population control or scientific experiment. But they certainly succeeded if a conspiracy was at work. Perhaps they had not bargained for such dramatic results.

# Aliens

Aliens are nearly always presented as harmless, rather clueless little green men. It is only very rarely that the possibility is presented that their intentions may not be entirely laudable, even in the light of the fact that their victims have all claimed to have been taken against their will and that they were completely powerless to protect themselves from various assaults. It cannot be denied that kidnapping, molestation and even rape are atrocious, even if the acts are committed by extraterrestrial beings with different social and moral codes from our own.

What is perhaps most disturbing is the considerable evidence pointing to the fact that the Western world's leaders are heavily involved with the aliens. This involvement would appear first and foremost to be military, which is disturbing at the best of times and, in non-wartime, downright sinister. Witnesses testify to the fact that particularly high numbers of UFOs are to be spotted around military bases all over the world, that there are military centers hidden underground all over the United States and that some people can even hear a disturbing buzzing sound in the southwestern U.S., which can only be caused by some massive underground project. What could the government be trying to hide? Why the need for massive security?

Can we really doubt that governments are capable of making a deal with an alien race? After all, why not allow these foreign races to take animals and humans for experiments, genetic engineering or any other purpose in exchange for technology going far beyond our own primitive scientific knowledge? Stories of abductions would suggest that aliens and those who deal with them have proved themselves to be far from trustworthy. Such actions are frightening and point to nothing less than a malevolent conspiracy.

Much UFO activity conveys a seemingly harmless program under the guise of exploration. By acting out a pretense of having no intention of domination, extraterrestrials feign what humans would term *conscience,* if a primitive conscience, of good and evil. And moreover, they are able to persuade our governments why they should work in cooperation together. They pile on the pathos and by claiming to be a physically weakened race who merely need to join their genetic makeup with a more developed human DNA structure to survive, they present a convincing tale that they have escaped from a dying planet and need the help of sympathetic foreigners. They thus manage to satisfy the humanitarian instincts in governments.

And so the saga continues and it would seem that we are heading towards inevitable catastrophe. Because as long as our governments continue in their naive gullibility, going along in their blindly altruistic beliefs that their deal with the aliens is mutually beneficial, the more leeway this gives the aliens. It would seem that the fate of our entire race, not to mention our planet, is at stake here. World domination by an extraterrestrial people is not an entirely comfortable prospect.

# Anti-Black

These days we like to believe that apartheid regimes do not exist in what we would call the developed world. But shocking stories of racial hatred abound from the areas of the world that we would think of as being most developed. It is in these areas that racism becomes most foreboding, because the technology is there to implement it. The possible manufacturing of AIDS is one manifestation, and possibly the most appalling one at that, but it is not the only one.

Many African-Americans believe that Charles Drew, the black Washington physician whose pioneering work with blood plasma saved thousands of lives, died after a car accident because he was denied entry into a whites-only hospital. A man whose work has benefited medicine for all races died because of racial prejudice.

While incidents such as this are shocking, the one thing that can be said in their favor is that they make no pretense at what they are setting out to do. What perhaps is even more shocking are the reports of conspiracies with the sole purpose of wiping out the black population in America. Sales of Tropical Fantasy, a soft drink produced by a firm

employing large numbers of ethnic minorities, fell dramatically after mysterious leaflets appeared in black areas
warning that the drink was actually a product of the Ku
Klux Klan and that it contained chemicals to sterilize black
men. Similar allegations arose over the Church's Fried
Chicken chain and the Snapple soft drinks. While the
AIDS virus has escalated out of all possible control, it
would seem that there are other, more small-scale projects
targeting the same victims.

# Area 51

For many years, speculation has gone on about what really takes place in a remote part of the Nevada desert. It seems somewhat strange that such a large expanse of land can be used to hide anything at all from public view, but it seems almost certain that something is taking place there that the public is not meant to know about.

The official line has it that the area is a military testing range. The only concrete information we have is geographical—we know that it is to the north of Las Vegas. Beyond that, we enter into a whole web of cover-up and conspiracy. Few people know what really goes on. Curtained off by a no-fly zone, it seems well-nigh impossible to glean any reliable information. The military seems to go to quite excessive measures to prevent any hope of entry. If the area is a military firing range, this is justifiable, but still, the entry prohibitions seem stringent to say the least. The area is fenced off, the fence being guarded by hundreds of closed circuit security cameras worthy of a modern-day Berlin Wall. Signs in the proximity warn that deadly force and violence is quite permissible to prevent intruders. Someone seems very keen to keep other people out. The roads surrounding the area are guarded by white vehicles bearing government plates. They are manned by men wearing black uniforms who appear to be heavily armed. Moreover, the roads are full of movement sensors which transmit any movement on the roads. All this does not seem to point to a conventional firing range.

And we just do not know what happens inside the area, because hardly anyone has been inside. All we know is that there is a large airbase which is not recorded on any map. Some intrepid explorers have risked their lives by photographing it from nearby hills and thus we do have photographic evidence of the airfield's existence.

One theory would have it that the area is a research center for investigating UFOs and for manufacturing the infamous black helicopters. Certainly, UFOs would need to be taken somewhere for investigation, such as in the aftermath of the Roswell incident. Of course, the American government could also be trying to reproduce the technology gleaned from the alien spacecraft here.

Cynics can pour cold water on the case of UFOs, but the case of black helicopters is indisputable. The American government's most deadly weapons have, for a long time, been kept secret to hide them from the view of potential enemies. Whatever the reason for the ominous black helicopters, it is quite clear that the public is deliberately kept in the dark about them.

An even more disturbing possibility is that some form of alien life is being kept alive in the area, retrieved from their spacecraft. Who knows what happened to the alien bodies after Roswell? If this is the case, it would seem that the authorities are sitting on a time bomb. The very fact the aliens have managed to come to Earth at all would suggest that their technology is far superior to ours. Which would, in turn, suggest that we cannot expect them to be subservient forever. Who knows how long it will be before the secret of Area 51 is revealed to us as the aliens break out of their confined space? There is without doubt something that we are not meant to see in there. The possibilities are horrifying.

# Army Exercises

Apparently, in recent years, Charlotte, North Carolina, has been victim to a terrifying series of military exercises posing under the guise of urban combat training. The town's inhabitants have been thrown into complete panic as gunfire and grenades have exploded in the dead of night. Hundreds of helicopters have come screeching down over residential areas, so low that they have rattled the windows of buildings not to mention the nerves of the people inside.

The police did not seem prepared to offer any reassurance at all and simply met inquiries with the response that "operations were being performed." The lighting conditions and tall buildings meant that Charlotte was an ideal location for the exercises to be carried out, unlike Fort Bragg, center of the U.S. Army's Special Operations Command. And the fact that the area was thinly populated and commercial meant that the setting was lifelike, without endangering civilians and soldiers. Or so the Army said.

But these excuses came over as distinctly pathetic to Charlotte residents who made their views on the unannounced exercises quite clear on local radio programs. As soon as the exercises began, Mayor Pat McCrory found himself inundated with telephone calls from citizens and staff as he himself attempted to take some control of the situation. Shortly afterwards he expressed his "deep concern" over the exercises in a letter to then President Clinton.

It turned out that the mayor was as much in the dark about the whole program as anyone else. He had been given no details about what would happen and the Army had simply ensured that they had his signature on the confidentiality agreement. Moreover, he was led to believe that there would be serious consequences if their plans were revealed to the public. Despite this, they let him imagine that their work was completely routine, that they would be in and out and no one would even know they were there.

But it would seem that the Army lied by what they did not say as much as what they did. Police Chief Dennis Nowicki of Charlotte-Mecklenburg was only given warning of the disruptions four hours before the start of the onslaught, and he was lucky to have been given any warning at all. He said "When you're holding back information, you're deceiving." And according to Malachi Greene, one of the city council members, "The city got hoodooed. . . . It's a deliberate thing on the part of these guys."

The Charlotte exercises were only one instance in a regular series of urban combat training exercises conducted by the Special Operations Command. Similar exercises have apparently been carried out in Pittsburgh, where nine helicopters and two hundred troops stormed the areas of McKeesport, the Strip District and Brighton Heights.

The harsh criticism from officials in the cities victim to the Army's exercises has not encouraged any willingness among the Special Operations Command to accept the well-being of local communities as something that needs to be taken into consideration. The military has, by law, the right to conduct training exercises as it sees fit. But to repeatedly ignore the vehement complaints of those affected by it does point to a conspiratorial pattern.

# Beast of Bodmin

Certain wildlife experts have admitted their fears in suggesting that a conspiracy at the highest level exists behind the British government's failure to admit the existence of the Beast of Bodmin.

A three-month study was carried out by top animal experts from the Ministry of Agriculture, Fisheries and Food, following complaints by local farmers. But the chairman of the National Register of Big Cat Sightings, Bob Engledow, believes that the study was inconclusive only because of hidden motives.

He says:

"There was no way that there was a genuine study. It was only done for a very short time over a very limited area. If they were genuinely looking they would have kept on for a couple of years right across the country. They obviously want to sweep up the queries as quickly as possible. I'm confident there's a cover-up by the government."

Government officials have denied these allegations. A representative for the Ministry said in response:

"We did it with the best experts available. We gave it our best shot. They weren't just going on a scouting mission with an elephant gun and a pair of binoculars. They went where there had been sightings and tracks found and unusual livestock deaths. We analyzed pictures and videos. We didn't do it as a great tracking-down exercise with great numbers of people sweeping the moor."

But Mr. Engledow said that it was in the government's interest not to find the beast.

"I think the government is worried about paying compensation to farmers who have lost livestock. It would have to pay because pumas and panthers escaped from captivity and the government should have caught them and not let them breed."

He goes on to add that hundreds of detailed sightings proved the big cats were loose in thirty-three counties. Moreover, if the government is not prepared to admit the existence of the Beast of Bodmin, how can we know what it is or is not hiding about the likes of the Loch Ness monster?

Of course, there is also the theory that the Beast of Bodmin is an alien in cahoots with the government. It might be a trifle embarrassing for the authorities to admit this at this stage, and might command a fundamental disrespect which would not stand them in terribly good stead at the next general election.

# Big Brother Is
# Watching You

Have you ever felt that THEY are watching you? Have you ever felt as if you are in the hands of the authorities, the plaything of a conspiracy about which you know nothing and over which you have no control? Not wanting to cast aspersions, suspicions or doubts onto our governments, here are some facts which may make you feel ever so slightly uncomfortable:

• Surveillance devices now in the hands of government officials include, according to MIT professor Gary Marx, "heat sensing imaging devices that can tell if a house is occupied, voice amplifiers, light amplifiers, night vision devices and techniques for reading mail without breaking the seal." Cameras can be concealed in virtually any piece of furniture.

• A major computer company is now marketing its "active badge" to employers. Employees attach this tiny gadget to their clothing and it gives out an emitting infrared beat every fifteen seconds. The movement is then picked up by strategically placed sensors and processed through a central computer, which means that employees can hide absolutely nothing from their bosses.

• On a typical day, four thousand telephone calls are legally recorded by authorities. How many calls are being eavesdropped on illegally? In some countries, every international phone call is recorded and monitored. Monitoring domestic calls is sometimes illegal, but with the (legal) development of microwave transmission, a huge number of long distance phone calls are now recorded.

• In April 1995, Great Britain opened the world's first DNA database. By the year 2000, five million Britons will have their genetic codes in the Home Office master computer. Under the current law, the Home Office has no right to anyone's genetic code unless they are a convicted criminal. The world of George Orwell's *1984* does not seem so far off, however, when the system can be expanded to collect records from citizens who not only haven't been convicted, but who have had no criminal dealings at all.

• The United States has the world's most extensive system of computer databases of personal information on citizens. The information is collected for purposes ranging from monitoring criminals to credit reporting to market research. The types of personal information collected on millions of Americans and stored in databases include the impersonal basics, such as names and addresses, but also completely invade an individual's privacy by storing such information as medical records, psychological profiles, drinking habits, political and religious beliefs.

• Electronic espionage has now become so common that few people even see it as a problem. Many networking software packages have worker-monitoring features built in as a matter of course. "Look in on Sue's computer screen," exhorts one ad for a major networking package. "Sue doesn't even know you're there!"

• According to a U.S. government study, the FBI's database of criminal histories is totally incomplete and inaccurate. Thousands of Americans are at risk of false arrest because of this.

• The number of people on the records of the criminal information system in California exceeds California's population.

• Over the last ten years, the FBI and other organizations have increased the amount of private mail they opened, read and inspected tenfold.

• The U.S. Customs Service plans a computer system that would classify incoming airline passengers as "high risk" or "low risk" based on information supplied by the airlines. The purpose is supposedly to speed up lines at customs counters. "Americans are meant to be free people. There're not supposed to be records made when you travel," said a skeptical U.S. representative. "The minute you get your name and birth date into a computer in Washington, watch out."

• It is a policy of the U.S. Navy to collect DNA samples on all new recruits. Who knows how long it will be before they start genetically engineering perfect sailors?

# Black Death

The first millennium A.D. over, the developed European world set off for pastures new and embarked on a massive new program of exploration and expansion. Explorers traveled far beyond the previously observed boundaries of Eastern Europe, and discovered new Eastern civilizations that not only had money but, in addition, were more than willing to trade. After several centuries, however, things started to turn sour and several of these Eastern nations grew discontented as they felt that their Western trade partners were taking advantage of them.

So the leaders of India took the initiative and set into motion a plan intended to all but annihilate the European nations. This became the first known case of biological warfare. Rats infected with a local plague were put on the ships of the European traders. The rats would then disperse through the port cities of the Mediterranean and as the Europeans would have no tolerance at all to the disease this would wreak complete havoc. Once this had happened, the Indians would march an army to Europe, knowing that the time required to march the distance would allow the plague to spread throughout Europe destroying huge numbers of the population. Once Europe was weakened by the plague, they could easily dominate and add vast new territories to their kingdom.

This plan only worked on one level. The Black Death, as it came to be called, certainly devastated entire nations as millions succumbed to the plague. But the Indians could not organize the army required to take Europe and thus their empire never spread.

# Black Helicopters

On May 7, 1994, a black helicopter pursued a teenage boy for forty-five minutes in Harrahan, Louisiana. Its exterior gave nothing away, bearing no mark of its origin or owners. The boy was terrified not as much by the sinister nature of the vehicle itself, but by the threatening stance of its occupants who had descended from the aircraft and pointed weapons at him. The boy has no idea to this day why the helicopter should have targeted him. The police chief was not forthcoming and intimated that the helicopters belonged to the American government, that in fact the matter was completely out of his hands.

A week later, people traveling in a car near Washington were given similar treatment. They too were chased, the helicopter following the car for several miles. They were completely unable to help themselves at all; when the driver tried to escape from the road, a rope ladder was let down and men in black uniforms and carrying weapons started to climb out. There was no option but to do as the men in the aircraft wanted. The driver counts himself lucky that the volume of traffic forced the aircraft to retreat in the end, but does not like to think what would have happened to him if the road had been deserted.

Then in 1995, a black helicopter flew over a couple's farm in Nevada. Spraying some unknown substance on the area, it had killed over a dozen of the animals by the next day, and months later, the surrounding vegetation was still clearly damaged. Official authorities denied any knowledge of the helicopter.

Mysterious black helicopters seem to be constantly in evidence, pursuing and terrifying completely innocent victims. They often seem to have some link to cattle mutilations and are seen in immediate proximity before, while or after they have taken place. What is most alarming is that the occupants of the helicopters do not even pretend to have peaceable intentions and are quite prepared to use gunfire and other violent means to their advantage, all the time keeping their identity secret.

The spraying of both urban and rural settings with unknown chemicals, and the killing of pets, plants and livestock for no apparent reason is more ominous still. Who knows whether the helicopters could be linked to the mysterious men in black, but people who have dared to photograph the helicopters have allegedly been accosted by men wearing black uniforms. They have then been told to leave the area and have been forbidden to tell anyone what has happened on pain of death. The men have also confiscated the cameras and film.

Whether the mysterious helicopters and their occupants are an alien phenomenon or whether they are in fact from hostile government departments we cannot know. But it seems certain that they do not come in peace and that they are not prepared to uphold fundamental democratic principles.

# Bormann

The death of Adolf Hitler has always been cryptic and many of the top Nazis are still unaccounted for. The fate of Hitler's deputy, Martin Bormann, is one of the unsolved mysteries of World War II, and, it would seem, has provided a role-model for Elvis Presley and Princess Diana. That said, he doesn't seem to have made too good a job of it and apparently he's been seen everywhere from Scandinavia to the Caribbean. And his body has never been found. While in 1972, a German court claimed to have found the skull of Bormann, some researchers say that it was no more than a ploy to put the Nazi hunters well off track.

Evidence from British intelligence officers has pointed to the fact that Bormann may have come to Britain after the War. Having the authority to release all German funds in Swiss banks, he was apparently brought to Britain and used by British intelligence to their advantage while being housed in a small village.

More bizarrely, the scheme to rescue Bormann was, apparently, conducted by Ian Fleming who, upon retirement from the British Secret Service, became the creator of

James Bond, who was to become the world's most famous secret agent.

Nevertheless, there are problems regarding this theory, not least of all that everyone involved is dead; Bormann apparently having died in the early '50s and Ian Fleming in 1964, not having breathed a word about the whole Bormann affair. But then, as the widow of one of Fleming's friends pointed out, "He maintained that you must never say anything more than you are morally bound to say."

# The British

Startling new evidence suggests that ever since the collapse of the North American empire, the British have sought to undermine and subvert the integrity of the U.S. On several occasions Britain has launched programs to regain its "lost colonies." What perhaps is most telling is its behavior during the early '60s, when it took advantage of the ever-increasing popularity of several musical ventures and formulated a grand scheme to corrupt the minds of the American youth in order to gain economic and cultural superiority over the nation. By means of careful marketing, British bands such as The Beatles, The Rolling Stones and The Who took the U.S. by storm.

Critics of this theory may reason that the effects of the "British Invasion" in the U.S. today are minimal. But perhaps more telling is the British attitude towards those cultural icons who have acted as diplomats for the greater good of the nation. This has included several knightings by the Queen. Perhaps the British impact in the U.S. may remain undetected to this day.

# Bruce Lee

B ruce Lee, dressed in the traditional Chinese outfit he wore in the movie *Enter the Dragon*, was laid to rest in Lakeview Cemetery in Seattle on July 20, 1973. But long before his sudden and tragic death at the age of thirty-two, rumors were rife throughout Asia that he had been dead for months. According to one source, Hong Kong Triads had killed Lee because he had refused to pay them protection money. Another claimed that he had been drugged by a former sensei who resented the fact that he taught martial arts to foreigners. Many Chinese people believe that Lee was the victim of his own rigorous training regime, while others cite drug abuse as the cause of his demise. It is even claimed by some cynics that Lee faked his death and that he is merely waiting for the right time to return to society.

The most popular story printed in the Hong Kong press suggested that the American Mafia had killed Lee. After completing the film *The Green Hornet*, Lee was approached by Mafia agents who wanted him to become the first Asian star in Hollywood. Bravely, Lee refused and returned home to Hong Kong. In the aftermath, it is alleged that humiliated

Mafia bosses signed Lee's death warrant and hired a professional assassin. An interesting postscript to this story claims that Lee's son Brandon, also a martial arts actor, was "accidentally" shot dead after he had found vital information about his father's killer.

Perhaps the most outrageous theory regarding Lee's death is that a prostitute killed him in a fit of panic. If the story is to be believed, Lee had taken a powerful aphrodisiac which had caused him to become very violent during sex. Fearing for her life, the prostitute reached out for the nearest heavy object—a glass ashtray—and struck Lee on the skull. He would never wake from the resulting coma.

Countless documentaries, books and magazines have purported to tell the "true" story of Bruce Lee's death. As far as the people of Hong Kong are concerned, the full facts surrounding Lee's passing have never been revealed, and probably never will be.

# Buns and Hot Dogs

One of the greatest conspiracies of the modern world is the fact that hot dogs come in packets of ten and hot dog buns come only in packets of eight. This may sound trivial, but when one starts to consider the marketing strategies involved, the amount of money being dealt with is quite staggering. Here's how it works.

You buy a packet of hot dogs and then you buy a packet of buns. Now you have two spare hot dogs and must buy another packet of buns to make up the difference. Now you have six loose buns . . . and so on and so forth. The two companies must have been in cooperation for some time now and have us all wrapped around their collective little fingers. Innocuous as it all may sound, when you consider the *billions* made by the two companies, it does make you wonder at what point they will strike collectively and take over the world.

# Cars

By the twentieth century, the U.S. had established its independence and England had accepted that even if they had lost their colonies, they had gained a powerful ally. However, a small number of British people could not cope with the idea of colonial independence. Ever since the War of 1812, conspirators devised elaborate scheme after elaborate scheme to return the colonies to English rule. After the Second World War, these thinkers devised a plan geared towards the collapse of the whole American infrastructure.

During the American boom years of the late 1940s through to the 1960s, the conspirators reached agreements with several British car manufacturers looking to expand their markets in the USA. Soon, brands such as MG, Triumph, Austin-Healey and Jaguar began to sell cars that were exquisitely beautiful, but nightmarishly finicky and unreliable to operate. The conspirators believed that the American roads, which, in the absence of an advanced public transport system, were so crucial to the running of the large nation, would grind to a halt as multitudes of English cars broke down and were left littering the surrounding countryside. The inevitable economic collapse that would follow would weaken the nation so much that an army of English soldiers could march into Washington and take over the nation.

Unfortunately, the English cars were so unreliable most didn't make it past the docks. Once the Americans realized what was happening they introduced safety regulations designed to bankrupt UK motor manufacturers. It worked!

# Cartoons

To some, children's animation is yet another form of not-so-subtle mind control. And so it was hardly a surprise when the connection between animation and mind control became quite literal. A somewhat bizarre incident in Japan, which induced nausea and epileptic-type fits in more than seven hundred children, provoked a wide-scale inquiry into the physical effects that television may have and the motives behind the inducement of these physical reactions.

It would appear that these convulsions were caused by a specific episode of a certain hit animation series, which had reached enormous popularity amongst the Japanese youth. A colorful explosion behind one of the popular characters used strobe lighting which seems to have stimulated nerve cells, causing seizures, breathlessness, impaired vision and nausea.

It would seem that strobe lighting produces an effect similar to hypnosis and that this was not the first time that screen addicts have suffered from epilepsy-type seizures. And electronic stimuli seem to be able to induce electrical charges in an individual's brain, again causing epileptic fits.

The question remains whether these cartoons, ever-popular among the Japanese young, could have used their harmless veneer as a disguise to experiment on their fans. The U.S. Pentagon has allegedly looked into the effects of strobe lighting to produce a nonlethal weapon, and Russia has apparently produced a computer virus going by the name of "666" affecting bodily functions by the same means.

# Chernobyl: Was It an Accident?

What actually happened? Was it an accident? Or were there in fact ulterior motives behind a conscious experiment?

More and more people are beginning to wonder if the latter proposition was in fact the case, and whether the Chernobyl disaster was not in fact the horrific accident it was made out to be but rather that it was consciously driven into an extremely dangerous situation on April 26, 1986. Chernobyl was certainly a situation known for its dangers, and the complete security mechanisms were left unobserved. The series of reported mistakes that went into the explosion are, to an extent, unbelievable. But why would the Soviet authorities have ordered such a large-scale disaster, devastating the lives of so many millions of people?

It has been suggested that the most likely explanation would be that the disaster constituted an experiment to prepare for fighting a nuclear war. If Chernobyl can ever make sense, one explanation could be that it would have been a logical starting point if Moscow was putting a plan for nuclear war against the West into action. If this was the case, it would have been necessary to test and conduct research into procedures and equipment that had been designed during the Cold War years to protect against radioactive contamination in the aftermath of nuclear war. Also, in order to be able to implement long-term protection, leaders would need to know about the immediate effects of the worst-case scenario. If a multiyear plan culminating in nuclear war against the West was in the cards, could a major nuclear disaster in the Ukraine have been a useful, if tasteless, preparatory experiment? The West has aided Russian scientists to gather a wealth of information about the short- and long-term effects of radioactivity. Furthermore, the most effective procedures have been developed to deal with the contamination, which will be of tremendous value if Moscow does act upon the rumors that are circulating.

Moreover, why should Russia be in the process of building a huge underground center in the Ural mountains? And the CIA's former acting director recently told military services in America that being prepared for nuclear war with Russia must remain a priority at all costs. Certainly Russia has been forced to modernize its nuclear infrastructure. We can only wait to see what will happen next.

# Christian Persecutions

By the time of Augustus's death in A.D. 14, the Roman Empire stood as by far the most influential political unit of the ancient world. Rome's religious tolerance must have been a central fact in this overwhelming political success. The Romans were not looking for trouble and only used persecution when absolutely necessary. Necessity included putting a stop to the suspected barbarism of the Druids and the activities of the Christians. The first Christian persecutions occurred during the reign of the emperor Nero who, after the fire of A.D. 64, declared that Christians were responsible for the arson. Persecutions continued in a fairly half-hearted way until the Trojan Dedius came into power in the third century, when authorities acting under the emperor's orders began a series of persecutions throughout the Empire. The number of persecutions began to increase, culminating in the reigns of Diocletian in the East and Maximianus in the West, when an Empire-wide manhunt for Christian blood began. Although most historians claim that the persecutions were simply due to a misunderstanding of the Christian religion, some researchers have suggested a more practical motive.

By the late third century, Rome's political prowess was under constant threat and, in order to be able to fight the competing nations, it urgently needed to control its increasingly unruly inhabitants. The Roman authorities searched for some distraction, something that would occupy the populace. The policy had already been put into action but relied on the cooperation of the slaves who participated in the events. During the third century Roman slaves increasingly revolted against their often violent destiny, much to the distress of the emperors, who recognized the public need for mass entertainment and so the Roman populace, now lacking an outlet for its pent-up frustrations, began taking to the streets in acts of violence. As a solution, the Christians, whose population in Rome was enormous, were used as unwitting sacrifices for Roman entertainment. In addition, their being burnt alive served to light Roman streets at night, bringing safety and warmth to the city. Witnessing the fate of the Roman Christians served its purpose of distracting the citizens and stabilizing the populace of Rome. Thus its continued survival was ensured into the third century. It was not until the reign of Constantine that Christianity was legalized and the persecutions stopped.

# Christopher Marlowe

In 1593 Christopher Marlowe, one of England's finest poets and dramatists, was stabbed to death by Ingram Frizer at the age of twenty-nine. Historians acknowledge that his murder was probably the result of a bar brawl—a dispute over who should pay the bill, in fact—but some people believe that his mysterious death may well have had a political cause. Prior to his death, accusations of blasphemy, subversion and homosexuality had destroyed his public image; he was also charged with atheism on the evidence of his former roommate and fellow dramatist, Thomas Kyd. As a result of his sacrilegious beliefs, some scholars allege that Marlowe was murdered by Francis Walsingham, a Puritan sympathizer and agent of Elizabeth I. Others accuse royalists, in particular the supporters of the Earl of Essex, of his murder. Significantly, Marlowe's killer eventually received a pardon from the Queen.

In the sixteenth century, the punishment for such crimes as Marlowe was accused of included being boiled alive, burnt at the stake, or hanged, drawn and quartered. Taking these penalties into consideration, it is hardly surprising that some people believe that Christopher Marlowe faked his own death. Had he simply fled the country, or gone into hiding, he would have been pursued as a fugitive for the rest of his life. A much better solution would have been to stage his own murder and assume a new identity. Having worked as a secret agent for years, Marlowe would have had both the experience and the contacts to hatch such a plan. Indeed, the fact that the coroner's inquest and subsequent burial of the body—in an unmarked grave—were completed within forty-eight hours of the "killing" gives even more credence to this idea.

To this day, conspiracy theories rather than facts shroud the events leading up to Marlowe's death. Though Ingram Frizer was named as the writer's killer, the real truth about Marlowe's end will probably never be known.

# Clinton

It goes without saying that former U.S. President Bill Clinton is not what he appears to be. But startling new evidence may point to the fact that he is neither a human nor an alien. Manufactured, patented and operated jointly by the FBI and a certain famous cartoon company, Bill Clinton is actually a robot.

Of course, it is only an indication of the superiority of current technology that he appears almost identical to a human and what is more, is able to fool people in everyday situations. He can, for example, communicate with others on his own. During his presidency his foreign policies were resolved by his creators, as are his domestic programs. Clinton's notorious sexual escapades only make him seem all the more human. What is more, the choice of Al Gore as his vice president served to make him look positively superhuman. Some right-wing groups became aware of the robotic nature of the former president. But the facts are so bizarre that they were reluctant to go public and risk their own heads, so they tried to bring him down by more conventional means. Clinton is rarely allowed out in the rain for fear of a short circuit.

# Coin Over Note

Maybe you have never noticed. Maybe you have tolerance of saintly proportions and maybe these things don't irritate you. But it has been pointed out that every time you buy something in a supermarket, the cashier will hand you your change, first with the notes and then the coins on top of them.

This means that unless you can perform some superhuman feat, you either have to crumple it all up into a ball or else perform the singularly pointless task of bringing your other hand over to separate the notes from the coins. And don't let yourself be persuaded into thinking that this is a mere logistical error. This is a conspiracy. They do it to annoy the hell out of you.

# David Kelly

Weapons expert Dr. David Kelly died in suspicious circumstances in July 2003 days after admitting to the Foreign Affairs Select Committee that he had spoken to BBC reporter Andrew Gilligan. The BBC subsequently reported that the danger Iraq posed had been exaggerated in the government dossier of September 2002, which warned the British public of the existence of certain weapons of mass destruction.

The Hutton Inquiry set out to determine whether or not the circumstances leading up to Dr. Kelly's death could have had an effect on his state of mind, or whether these circumstances might have influenced the actions of others. Yet in a statement delivered by Lord Hutton on January 28, 2004, the following ruling was made: "I am satisfied that Dr. Kelly took his own life by cutting his left wrist and that his death was hastened by his taking Co-Proxamol tablets. I am further satisfied that there was no involvement by a third person in Dr. Kelly's death."

The forensic pathologist at the Hutton Inquiry, Dr. Nicholas Hunt, judged that Dr. Kelly bled to death from a cut to the wrist, but other experts were skeptical of this conclusion. In a letter to the *Guardian,* medical specialists David Halpin, C. Stephen Frost and Searle Sennett expressed their view that this was "highly improbable." Dr. Hunt stated that only the ulnar artery had been completely transected. This complete transection would cause the artery to retract and close down, enabling the blood to clot. To have died this way Dr. Kelly would have had to lose much more blood than the ambulance team reported.

Alexander Allan, the forensic toxicologist at the inquiry, said that the blood level of the drug's components was less than a third of what is normal for a fatal overdose. Halpin, Frost and Sennett conclude their letter by stating: "We dispute that Dr. Kelly could have died from haemorrhage or from Co-Proxamol ingestion or from both." This theory raises the question of the real cause of Dr. Kelly's death—and, furthermore, why it is not being made known to the public.

Dr. Kelly denied that he could have been the BBC's main source and the Ministry of Defence claimed that no suggestion was made that Dr. Kelly should lose his job over the issue. However, a friend of Dr. Kelly, British diplomat David Broucher, told the Hutton Inquiry that in an e-mail hours before his disappearance, Dr. Kelly hinted at his crisis with lines such as "many dark actors playing games." In other conversations, Kelly seemed to predict his own death, saying that he would "probably be found dead in the woods" if the British invasion of Iraq was to go ahead.

# Diana 1: Dodi

The hysteria has died down. The public mourning has abated. And conspiracy theories are running rife. Paparazzi? Or was there a more malevolent motive behind Diana's death?

Speculations that Diana was killed by MI5 were raised the very night she died, and over the next two crucial weeks, various distinct themes began to emerge. One was that she was killed by the royal family or, acting on the royals' behalf, the British intelligence. Their reasoning? They did not want a Muslim, in the figure of Dodi Al-Fayed, to act as stepfather to the future King of England. Or alternatively, Charles wanted to be free to marry his long-time confidante and love, Camilla Parker-Bowles. Certainly the BBC reported that the Libyan leader told his followers in a televised speech that the "accident" was a combined French and British conspiracy, because they did not want an Arab man to marry a British princess.

The drunk driver and the paparazzi were all part of the masterplan, so the theory goes. Other suggested conspirators include the IRA, the CIA, Islamic Militants and even the Freemasons. After all, Diana and Dodi were killed under a stonework bridge, a Masonic symbol.

There is the theory that Diana was killed by agents of international arms manufacturers to stop her crusade against land mines. And yet another version has it that she faked her own death, Elvis-style, and that she and Dodi are now living on a deserted island somewhere far away from the paparazzi. Along with JFK.

There are, furthermore, those who believe that the accident was faked by a random alien spacecraft so they could transport Diana up to their ship to be with Elvis. But again, that would have been no mean feat. Who really was responsible for the events of August 1997?

# Diana 2: Closed Casket

One theorist has commented how significant it was that Mother Theresa lay in state in a big glass coffin compared to the closed casket of Princess Di. Dodi's casket has never even been seen, let alone open at a funeral.

The story goes that their faces were too badly damaged for open casket viewing but then, we're also told that Diana was uttering some final words.

Naturally, the bounds of taste would dictate that it might not be entirely appropriate to have the public hordes ogling Diana's corpse, but has anyone seen *any* dead bodies? Is there really a religious reason for Dodi to have been buried straight away?

One piece of evidence supporting this theory is that bodyguard Trevor Rees-Jones is still alive, despite claims from Mercedes experts that it would have been well-nigh impossible for anyone to have survived a crash in a car going at 121 miles per hour. Maybe, as Henri Paul's lawyers claim, the car was not going that fast. Maybe the crash was in fact faked by Rees-Jones who had previously deposited Diana and Dodi elsewhere?

More and more bizarrely, Dodi's usual driver was not

used. The mystery of Henri Paul, the security officer who only agreed to drive the vehicle at the last minute, is still unsolved. His identity was kept undercover for several days after the crash. According to colleagues at the Ritz Hotel, he had been something of a loner and did not socialize with them. Such little personal information seems to exist on Paul that one version of the story would have it that Henri Paul simply did not exist, another that he was whisked away from the hospital after being pronounced dead by doctors working with the Al-Fayed family.

Perhaps most suspiciously of all, Di let it slip to the *Daily Mail* just six hours before she died that she was going to withdraw completely from public life. Well, she certainly did that. Whether the crash was an impressive "death" scene from which she retreated into blissful privacy, or whether it was an attempt at a faked death that went horribly wrong, we don't know. Plastic surgery permitting, it might be worth looking out for a stunningly attractive "nanny" coming to visit Diana's children.

## Diana 3: MI6

If Di was a threat to the throne, she was, many would say, a threat to the stability and well-being of the state. What better reason for elements of the Secret Service to wipe her out? Some members of the Secret Service seem to have a somewhat odd idea of what constitutes a threat to the state. Files exist on John Lennon and on Jack Straw, and they once tried to destroy the entire Labour government of the 1970s. It is not outside the realms of possibility that the same organization who believed that Lennon was capable of wreaking social and political havoc also believed that Diana was about to stir up widespread popular unrest.

What is more, MI6 were suspected of bugging Diana throughout her married life, hounding her and then releasing personal information. For example, many believe that it was they who were behind the release of "Squidgygate" that so damaged her reputation during the breakup with Charles.

Bodyguard Trevor Rees-Jones had once been a member of the Parachute Regiment and had completed two spells in Northern Ireland. He had also served in the Royal Military Police. With this kind of background, it would have been almost impossible not to have come into contact with members of the Secret Service. Could the fact that only he survived the crash be evidence of the fact that he was involved in the plot to kill Diana?

# Diana 4: The Dodi Target

There is also the theory that Diana's death was brought about not by a plot to kill her, but rather as a result of an elaborate plan to assassinate Dodi by business enemies of his father. Certainly, the death of Diana would have been a spectacular cover-up for any such operation.

Mohammed Al-Fayed has made more than a few enemies in his time. His acquisition of Harrods came about only after a bitter battle, and he was denied British nationality after questions were raised about his business negotiations and other activities. As his oldest son, Dodi would have been an obvious target for anyone wanting to right the balance with Al-Fayed.

# Diana 5: The Egyptian Point of View

The Egyptian press would have it that Egyptians are under constant threat from foreigners. Their morals and economy are undermined and corrupted and their Moslem faith is constantly challenged and subverted. It is not surprising that most of the time the finger is pointed at their old rival, Israel. The Israelis are accused of infecting the Egyptian young with AIDS, and accusations have even extended to the Israelis flooding the Egyptian markets with aphrodisiac chewing gum in what would appear to be a rather pathetic attempt at mind control. Egypt's semi-obsession with conspiracy theories may seem to be rather paranoid, but it is not entirely without foundation. The history of the Middle East is full of compelling conspiracies ranging from the palace goings-on of the Ottoman era to Israel's botched attempt to assassinate a Hamas leader by injecting him with an exotic poison.

Many Egyptians, moreover, were put out to find that Mohammed Al-Fayed had been refused citizenship to Britain and felt that the media reports placing his son's death completely in the shadow of that of Diana only served to contribute to the general hostility against their race. Within days of the accident, conspiracy theories had surfaced in Egypt. Columnist Anis Mansour wrote in Egypt's leading English-language newspaper, *al-Ahram Weekly*, "British intelligence killed her to save the throne, just as the CIA killed Marilyn Monroe at the same age. When it turns to marrying a Muslim from whom she might have borne a boy named Mohammed or a girl named Fatemah and that Muslim child would be the brother of the King of England, the guardian of the church, there had to be a solution."

"Who killed her?" asked an account of "Diana's Conversion to Islam" in *al-Ahram*. "British intelligence? Israeli intelligence? Or both? We believe that Diana's conversion to Islam was the reason she was killed. Hadn't she said she was going to shock the world?"

And yet some Egyptian commentators have mocked all the sensation-mongering. The *al-Ahram Weekly* does comment on the failure of one such author to "implicate the French company that first built the tunnel into the murder."

# Doctors

Doctors may say that they are working to make you better. But then they only make money if they make sure that you stay ill. So why would they want to make you healthy?

It seems that if they get rid of illness, they get rid of doctors. And the way they keep the public money rolling in is quite simple really. First of all, in the name of biological research, they will invent the cure for a disease. Then they invent the disease itself and let it loose to go its merry way killing thousands of people. Of course, they need millions of dollars per month to try to find a cure even though they know what the cure is. Their next step all depends on how much damage the disease is causing. But that is only of secondary importance; more vital is how much money it is bringing in. At some stage, they announce that they have found the cure. Everyone gets very excited but then they say that they were wrong and that actually they need further millions of dollars per month to find the real cure.

The money keeps rolling in and after a few more years, they release a new disease and the whole process is set into motion again. They push it into the main spotlight and quietly cure the first disease. This solves the problem of why there are so many different diseases around at any one time. These big corporations of doctors make billions every month by using innocent victims as prey to their superplot.

Bearing this in mind, it seems really quite obvious that all doctors are actually working from an extraterrestrial headquarter, or maybe they are simply humans working for aliens. It would thus follow that their manufacturing of disease is in fact only a further pretence. Alien parasites are enough to make anyone feel queasy so what better way to infect large numbers of the population? Just to prove the point, when was the last time a doctor was able to explain anything in any sort of language that mere mortals might understand? And think about their handwriting. When was the last time you ever saw anyone else claiming to be educated pass off such absolute scribble? It must be quite hilarious for them when we can't understand them speaking in alien dialect, but we nod our heads and pretend we do all the same.

So next time a doctor bombards you with alien-speak, it might throw him off his guard just to let him know that you know exactly what he is doing. Something along the lines of "Look, I'm not going to understand, so just give me the drugs and bleed my financial resources completely dry." You never know, it might scare him a little. Or at least ruin his fun.

# Drugs

In *Brave New World*, Aldous Huxley depicts a totalitarian regime where the government maintains their power by inflicting drugs on their citizens. The novel has a futuristic setting, but the reality that it depicts may not be so far from the truth.

Andrew Cooper, the publisher of the Brooklyn weekly newspaper *The City Sun*, puts forward the theory that white middle class communities push heroin into the black communities to divert the young from political activity. And it would seem that this situation is not unique to the African-American communities. Senator John Kerry of Massachusetts carried out an investigation into what he saw as the drug conspiracy, concluding that the CIA and the U.S. government knew about and participated in cocaine smuggling in cahoots with Nicaraguan drug barons, as part of an elaborate ploy to overthrow the former left-wing government of Nicaragua.

Rumors that the American government is dumping drugs in black neighborhoods go back at least to the Vietnam War years. Then, heroin was allegedly promoted to stop the increasing militancy within the black community across the nation. Political black activist Dick Gregory says that "Nothing in the history of the planet is as vile as what we're about to uncover. As bad as slavery was, white folks never accused us of jumping on the boat." But, he said, black people have been blamed for the uprising of drugs.

# Earthquakes

Earthquakes are an example of Mother Nature's most destructive natural disasters. They have left a trail of devastation across the globe and throughout the centuries. But could it be that more recent seismic activity is the product of man and not of the earth?

In the deep recesses of the Alaskan tundra U.S. intelligence are working on a new weapon for the twenty-first century. Known as Project HAARP (High-Frequency Active Auroral Research Program), the project is described as the world's largest "ionospheric heater." It transmits high-frequency radio waves into the ionosphere, sending more than a gigawatt of energy into the sky. The official explanation for this project from the U.S. Navy is that it is "to observe the complex natural variations of Alaska's ionosphere." This could lead to advances in communications technology, enabling transmissions to be sent over enormous distances and underground.

But independent analysts believe this is a pretext concealing the true nature of the project, which is to develop new technologies enabling human manipulation of weather patterns, mind control and man-made earthquakes. In his book, *HAARP: The Ultimate Weapon of the Conspiracy,* Jerry E. Smith predicts that these experiments may have far graver consequences than people realize. The HAARP project involves detecting and observing electromagnetic activity, which is the catalyst for seismic activity and movement amongst the Earth's tectonic plates. This technology could be harnessed by the military to trigger earthquakes, either deliberately or by accident. The science behind this is so complex that unless those working on it fully comprehend it they could create an unexpected disaster.

Man can already instigate seismic activity through five known techniques: injecting fluids into the earth at extremely high pressures; extracting fluids already underground; mining activity and quarrying; testing nuclear weapons; and constructing artificial barriers like dams and reservoirs. Scientists agree that there have been man-made earthquakes already. In Denver during the 1960s there were several earthquakes of varying intensity which coincided with waste disposal schemes that involved injecting waste deep underground. This high pressure injection of waste triggered the release of stored strain energy in the underground rock, causing the destruction of several blocks of suburban Denver.

The exploitation of the HAARP technology could prove vital for the Pentagon. In the future if they wanted to create instability in a region, instead of using conventional military capability, they could manipulate an area using geophysical weapons. According to Professor Gordon MacDonald, "The key to geophysical warfare is the identification of environmental instabilities to which the addition of a small amount of energy would release vastly greater amounts of energy." Just tiny amounts of energy could spell catastrophe, especially in poor regions of the world with an inferior infrastructure and shoddily constructed buildings. The blame for these events would appear to lie with Mother Nature and not with the real culprits.

The implications of this are enormous. All future disasters could potentially be created by covert military planners. With secrecy of the project being imperative, the real cause of these events could be undetectable to the outside world.

# Ebola

Conspiracy theories about outbreaks of Ebola in Zaire are running as rife as the disease itself. Ebola is a virus that incubates inside its human hosts in less than two weeks, turning internal organs to pulp and causing severe blood clots, hemorrhaging and brain damage. Moreover, it is incurable.

Theories parallel suspicions that AIDS is a man-made killer designed to eliminate the world's "useless eaters." Could outbreaks of Ebola have been engineered? Could the U.S. military, or the New World Order, or the United Nations or the Center for Disease Control have developed a lethal virus to expunge those aforementioned useless eaters? Or to develop a worldwide epidemic? Some theorists have noticed that the Center for Disease Control in Atlanta has brought back samples of the lethal virus. Whatever the truth, population control seems at its most drastic here.

# Echelon

Those living in the Western world have become accustomed to increasing openness and democracy in their governments throughout the last decades of the twentieth century and the beginning of the twenty-first, but in one area there remains profound secrecy and confidentiality: the role of spies. Governments' reticence to discuss all matters, both significant and trivial, relating to our security services has created an aura of suspicion and of illicit or clandestine operations carried out in our name.

At the heart of people's fears is the question of just whom the MI5 and MI6 may be spying upon. Next time you make a phone call, send an e-mail, telex or fax, be careful what you say and write because someone could be eavesdropping. Despite the implementation of privacy and human rights laws in many countries, rumors have continued for several years that there is an enormous electronic surveillance machine intercepting all international communications traffic across the world, and processing it through giant supercomputers. These rumors have persisted since the beginning of the Cold War, but in the 1980s formal proof of this Orwellian scheme emerged. It was intelligence chiefs in New Zealand whose consciences forced them to admit what had been going on for a generation. A system called ECHELON had been developed following an agreement known as the UKUSA treaty, signed in 1947, between the governments of the United States, the UK, Canada, Australia and New Zealand.

This alliance aimed to create a global intelligence network with a vast pool of information for analysis by the security services of the treaty's signatories. Although it is illegal for the British and American security services to spy on their respective citizens and companies, the members of the alliance managed to neatly sidestep national laws by spying on each other. So, for example, if MI6 wanted to spy on a suspect individual in London, rather than go through the lengthy process of applying for a warrant, they could simply get their American counterparts to do it for them, and then share the information.

The system was designed by America's National Security Agency, who have access to all of the information, however, the other members may only view the certain sectors of the collected intelligence relevant to their particular spheres of influence. The centerpiece of the whole operation is the ECHELON dictionary, a vast resource of keywords, including names, subjects, locations, telephone numbers and e-mail addresses. The millions of daily communications around the world are automatically scanned to pick up recognized words, phrases, numbers and addresses. Every match is then transcribed and used by intelligence gatherers.

The system has already provoked the ire of European Union countries that are not members of the pact. The issue was so sensitive that a European Parliament report was commissioned to look into the affair. "It is a very dangerous attack on the sovereignty of member states," complained one MEP. The French government is angered by what it believes is illegal tapping of government and business communications, with information shared solely amongst ECHELON allies. The European report cited "wide-ranging evidence" that information is used "to provide commercial advantages to companies." The French press has made claims that Boeing was provided secret information to deprive Airbus, its European rival, of contracts.

Conceivably, this system has significant uses in combating terrorism, crime and threats to national security, but its implications for civil liberties and it's dubious legal authority raise vital questions for citizens and politicians. The lack of formal acknowledgment of its existence, or its precise composition and function, inspires those with conspiratorial minds to question just precisely what is going on.

# Eiffel Tower

History would have us believe that the Eiffel Tower, the archetypal symbol of Paris, was the brainchild of Burgundian Gustave Eiffel, and that it was built as an exhibition showpiece. It is kept quiet, with just cause, that the structure is actually the product of a pro-German architect and that it was part of a long-term plot geared towards the eventual conquest of France.

The Tower, built under the guise of a World Fair's centerpiece, was actually intended as a Zeppelin mooring mast. The placement of the tower in the middle of the capital city of France was ideal, as it would allow troops to descend into the heart of Paris itself, thus ensuring a quick and easy takeover when the time arrived.

It goes without saying that this plan was never put into action, but who knows who or what will land on the Eiffel Tower in the future?

# Elvis

Most people are only aware of one side to Elvis Presley. Most of us are unaware that he was in fact an agent for the CIA. And most of us are blind to the implications of this.

Elvis's rise in popularity provided the perfect cover for a top-secret military installation in the heart of Memphis, Tennessee. The fact that the site was so high profile meant that the CIA officials could be as open as they wanted as it was thought that no one, internal or foreign, would ever suspect an international celebrity's home as a headquarters for an international spy network. However, obviously some precautions had to be taken and to prevent a suspicious number of government vehicles congregating in Elvis's driveway, an extensive system of tunnels were dug, some extending for several hundred yards. At Agent Presley's death, the government took precautionary measures to ensure that the mansion remained within the Presley family. Rumor has it that, despite the constant waves of tourists, the tunnel network is in continuous use.

# Elvis Killed Kennedy

Quite apart from his underhand dealings with the CIA, there seems to be another side to Elvis that is generally unknown. The suggestion that Elvis may have killed charismatic President John F. Kennedy for having hogged the media coverage is not to be missed. It would seem that a whole chain of events was triggered by this event and that a network of conspiracies can be unraveled by examining it.

If Elvis killed Kennedy, the question remains as to who killed Elvis. And if jealousy over media coverage was one reason for the assassination, it would make sense that John Lennon was overcome by a similar pique of jealousy and killed Elvis to make way for his own publicity.

And the theory does not stop there. It would seem that Lennon did not think ahead very far and see that Elvis was influential. The theory alleges that the tragic assassination of John Lennon in 1980 might have been performed by Elvis supporter Michael Jackson, who, in turn, closed the circle of conspiracy and gave the whole thing away by marrying Elvis's daughter, Lisa Marie Presley. The celebrity world is nothing if not incestuous.

# Fluoride

Strong bones and teeth, but at what cost? Unnamed sources have revealed information regarding the mass fluoridation conspiracy in Westernized countries. Could the addition of this powerful chemical to our drinking system be wreaking havoc on our people? There is a distinct possibility that information is being withheld from the public in a massive cover-up.

There is no denying that fluoride does initially strengthen bones and teeth. But the benefits are short-lived. There comes a point when genetic damage erupts. Bones are weakened to the point of complete dissolution. Within seven generations, offspring of fluoridated reproduction are born without any skeleton at all.

This theory provokes the serious concern that there is a dreadful fate in store for the entire Western world. Furthermore, the question is raised of whether the potentially dire consequences were known when fluoride was introduced into our water. Could this be yet another disturbing attempt to curb population growth?

# Franklin

The years immediately following the American Revolution were not stable ones for the new United States of America. England had a long history of power behind it as well as huge amounts of support from allied countries, but the United States was, at that stage, too newly established to encourage the interests of the nations of Continental Europe. In addition, the new nation did not have strong military resources and was certainly not in the position to protect its extensive coastline. Although they had gained their independence from England, the Americans knew only too well that the English crown was in a stronger position than they were and that if they chose to retaliate, the consequences could be fairly bleak for them. .

American leaders were anxious to protect their own interests as-well as the interests of the nation and realized that friendship with one of the major European nations would be significantly beneficial. France had already sent over troops, ships and money to aid the cause of the Revolution and, having been long-term foes of England as well as an established nation in themselves, the Americans realized that France would make an ideal partner in terms of what they both wanted. However, they also realized that the French were inclined to be fickle. To prevent the collapse of United States/French relations, the leaders of the nation hit upon a plan.

Benjamin Franklin, the internationally renowned scientist and politician, was called to serve as an American ambassador to France. Franklin was himself a man of remarkable talents. Plans were set into motion whereby he would use his charm to impress the French ladies as much as possible. They would respond, and a Franco-American tribe could be fathered by Franklin.

In this way, the Americans secretly hoped that these descendants would continue the alliance between the two nations in a way that was mutually beneficial. Unfortunately, however, the French Revolution of 1789 put a stop to this. The beheading of the pro-American monarch Louis XVI and many members of the French aristocracy did not improve Franco-American relations and the government which followed the French Revolution and the rise of Napoleon Bonaparte would not take so kind an attitude towards the new nation.

# Grand Conspiracy

We all know that the government would like us to believe that what they propagate is true. And we all know that it is very probably not true. And hence we quite rightly take what the government says with a little pinch of salt. But . . . suppose it is not the government itself that is at fault? Suppose that the government actually believes what it is telling us and that it is in fact controlled by a clandestine super-government who manipulates its every move?

The thought that all the presidents of the world are no more than the plaything of some giant power-maniac may seem uncomfortably close to the aims of Saddam Hussein, and the thought that there really is some dictatorial Saddam-type figure behind it all is a little worrying. Because if such a figure or an organization has controlled leading world governments, they are pretty much on line to conquer the world.

What is most frightening is that such a conspiracy just cannot be proven. Small conspiracies are only finite in their power and once they are uncovered their power is diffused, but such all-encompassing scenarios as this defy, by their very nature, being proved. Any lack of evidence simply goes to prove the superiority of the cover-up, while any attempt at disagreement is a clear manifestation that you are one of the conspirators. And when it comes down to it, it would be completely impossible to actively disprove the existence of alien visitors or Men in Black or UFOs simply by lack of evidence. On the other hand, there is no evidence to prove the existence of Flower Fairies, and it would seem quite easy to disprove them.

# Gulf War Cover-Up

During the 1990s Gulf War, the world was astounded at the superiority of the American war effort. Iraqi armies were overtaken by a ratio of about a thousand to one. The troops came back alive.

But that is not to say that they came back healthy, and thousands of war veterans have died or are dying from what has commonly come to be known as Gulf War Syndrome. Scientists' attempts to locate the precise origins of Mycoplasma Incognita are not helped by the government's unbending denials that there is such a thing as Gulf War Syndrome in the first place.

It is thought that Mycoplasma Incognita could have been manufactured as a sort of biological warfare agent. Whoever created this weapon allegedly used the HIV gene and so the illness therefore targets those with weak immune systems. But no one seems to know what the real story is. Lack of funding, as well as pressure from the government to cover up what has really gone on, has hampered extensive research. It would seem that the M. D. Anderson Cancer Center is the only center where this is being taken seriously.

In recent years the government has released documents which suggest that Gulf War veterans are indeed right when they claim that they were exposed to chemical and biological agents during Operation Desert Storm, a claim which had previously been denied over and over again. Supporters of the veterans have claimed that the U.S. was directly responsible for the weapons in the first place, having sold those chemical and biological agents to the Iraqis.

And it would appear that the veterans might have been used as test subjects by the military themselves. The military, it would seem, forced the troops to take injections of experimental drugs which were supposedly intended to protect them from biological weapons and nerve gas. Immediately prior to the Gulf War, the U.S. Food and Drug Administration adopted the Interim Rule which allows the military to use experimental drugs on military staff without their consent "during times of military exigency." The Interim Rule is still being observed. As a result, the troops were given shots of pyridostigmine bromide tablets and botulism toxoid vaccine. The FDA maintained that the military provide staff with information about the side effects of these experimental drugs and demanded that thorough records be kept of which troops they were administered to.

This, according to the National Gulf War Resource Center, however, is not the case. The Department of Defense failed to inform troops of the possible side effects and virtually forced them into taking the injections. The Department of Defense also failed to keep records of which troops were given experimental drugs and did not keep complete records of the side effects that were inevitably experienced by the troops. This lack of recordkeeping hinders veterans' ability to get medical help to this day.

What is most frightening is that Mycoplasma Incognita seems to be highly contagious. It is claimed that some of the families of these Gulf War veterans have now been attacked by the disease and low-income families who were given surplus Desert Storm food at food banks may also have become ill.

Could this be a warped form of population control? Starting with men and women who pledged their lives to serve their country and who now can't get enough help from the authorities who sent them out in the first place?

# Guy Fawkes and the Gunpowder Plot

On November 5, 1605, thirty-six barrels of gunpowder were found in a cellar beneath Parliament in London—part of a conspiracy to bring down the English government and King James I. Although the plot was the brainchild of one Robert Catesby, Guy Fawkes was pegged as the mastermind of the plan, purportedly protesting against the religious persecution of Catholics in England. Theories concerning motives are widespread, but most historians believe that the plotters planned to assassinate the King, raise a popular rebellion and restore a Catholic monarch to the throne.

The full facts surrounding the discovery of the plot are unclear and a number of theories exist as to how the conspirators were foiled. Popular belief has it that a letter was sent to the Catholic Lord Monteagle, warning him of the plot and advising him not to attend the Opening of Parliament. The suspected writer of the letter was Francis Tresham, Monteagle's brother-in-law, who had been invited to join the "terrorists" but had declined. On receiving the letter, Monteagle allegedly informed the Earl of Salisbury. In the early hours of November 5, a search party was sent into the Parliament cellars, where they discovered Fawkes and his cache of gunpowder.

One alternative theory suggests that Salisbury became aware of the plot some time before the warning was sent—the "Monteagle Letter" may have been fabricated by government officials in order to frame the conspirators. After discovering the plot, government officials then let it develop, with the aim of catching the group red-handed.

On January 31, 1606, Fawkes and his co-conspirators were publicly executed at Westminster, the very building they had intended to blow up.

# Harry Potter

Of the thousands of column inches and hundreds of broadcast hours devoted to the phenomenally successful series of J. K. Rowling's Harry Potter books, only a scarce few have claimed the influence of the occult within this remarkably popular set of books.

The fifth installment, *Harry Potter and the Order of the Phoenix*, contains exactly 666 pages (excluding the prologue). The book's worldwide release date was at midnight on the eve of the Summer Solstice. Although cynics would suggest this was a simple marketing gimmick, there was no reference made to the unusual timing of the launch in the promotional campaign.

Many studies on the Harry Potter series have noted various symbolic connections. The lightning scar by which Harry is recognized is a symbol used in Satanism. Unicorns, which are featured in the series, are symbolic of the Antichrist. The Phoenix is said to be Lucifer, who was cast down in flames and will rise again triumphantly. Mandrake plants resembling humans are grown and used for medicinal purposes, leading some people to draw comparisons with human sacrifice. Some believe these connections are made deliberately to confuse the young mind. However, 60 percent of Harry Potter books are purchased for adults to read, which may suggest that an interest in the occult has a much wider grip on society than was previously realized.

# Hatshepsut

The temple of ancient Egypt ruler Hatshepsut at Deir El-Bahri, across the Nile from Thebes, is dated from the fourteenth century B.C. and serves as evidence of her success as the longest reigning female pharaoh Egypt ever had. Credit for this achievement would not be given for the best part of the millennia and a half for which the monument has stood.

Born in approximately 1503 B.C. to the respected Pharaoh Thutmose I, Hatshepsut had two brothers and one half-brother, Thutmose II, who was also her husband. When her brothers died, Hatshepsut had only one contender to the throne: her young nephew, Thutmose III, the offspring of her husband's other wife, Isis.

Owing to the youth of her nephew, Hatshepsut reigned as dowager queen, but, unwilling to give up her sovereignty when Thutmose III came of age, Hatshepsut donned the title of king . . . as well as the clothes and beard to match. This worked, keeping her in power for around fifteen to twenty years.

After Hatshepsut's death, her mummy was stolen and her tomb destroyed—only a canopic jar containing her liver was ever found. Similarly, the hard stone sarcophagus of Senmut, her advisor, architect and lover, was found in more than twelve hundred pieces. All cartouches formally bearing her name were scratched out and replaced with that of a Thutmose. This was easily done, since any image of her was bearded. It is thought that these destructive acts, and possibly the deaths themselves, were the work of Hatshepsut's frustrated and jealous nephew on reaching an age when he should have been in power.

For centuries historians were baffled by the mystery of the Thutmoses, who apparently ruled in a muddled order, but these revealing theories have lifted the lid on an age-old conundrum.

# Hitler Assassination Plots

Only very recently have the plots to assassinate Adolf Hitler been finally uncovered. Operation Foxley, as it is called, has, for the first time, been released to the Public Record Office in Kew, West London. The detailed 120-page manuscript tells of how plans for an assassination attempt were laid out by the Special Operations Executive who dealt with operations behind the enemy lines. These propositions ranged from plans for individual attack (for which a potential assassin had even been targeted) to a full-blown SAS bombing on Hitler's mountain hideaway. Other possible approaches for the action included bringing Rudolph Hess, Hitler's deputy, to England, hypnotizing him and sending him back to Germany to kill SS chief Heinrich Himmler.

Plans started with investigating Hitler's daily routine down to the smallest possible details, so that the best strategy could be planned. Poisoning his tea was one possibility considered, using a chemical called "I" with a delayed action that would give an attacker the time to flee. Hitler being extremely fond of apple juice, it was also suggested that "I" could be added to this, as it would not change either its taste or appearance.

It was considered that the best opportunity for attack was mid-afternoon, as Hitler walked to his teahouse in his hideaway in the Bavarian Alps. The assassins would be disguised in German military uniforms and would carry high-explosive grenades for self-protection. This would involve getting through a wire fence and avoiding German dog controls.

Another possibly less direct method on the part of the SOE was to circulate details of the sexual antics of the top Nazis in an attempt to wreak havoc behind the enemy lines. The theory was that if the concentration camp atrocities were not enough to shock the enemy, perhaps more graphically sexual horror stories would galvanize them into some kind of action. Tidbits of gossip were circulated to give the German public the impression that their leaders were involved in ongoing orgies. The Nazi Party chief in Munich, Christian Weber, was attacked particularly ferociously here. He was reputed to be famous for parties in which a naked girl would be strapped to a roulette wheel. The wheel was placed on a table and the Nazi officials sat around it. Once the wheel stopped, the gentleman sitting opposite would prove his virility to the assembled company. "A good time was had by all," apparently, but this view skirts the issue of the girl's unconsciousness by the end of the session.

Some senior figures in the Special Operations Executive, however, believed that Hitler's capacity for tactical ineptitude in his war effort meant that he was in fact better alive than he was dead. The danger if he was killed would be that, far from acting as a catalyst to the end of the war, the whole German war strategy would in fact be improved. There was also the danger that once dead the German dictator would be worshipped by his public and be canonized into a martyr's role.

# Hitler's Staged Provocations

Hitler's rise to power in Germany displays a remarkable manipulation of events to develop and explain evil objectives. The Reichstag Fire of February 27, 1933, is a prime example of such behavior. Although it is unclear who actually started the fire, it is undeniable that the Nazis capitalized on the event and manipulated it entirely to their own advantage. Claiming that the fire was a left-wing onslaught against the established state, Hitler persuaded President Hindenburg to sign a decree "for the Protection of the People and of the State." This enabled the state to exercise whatever powers it so wanted in the name of public safety. Certain crimes became punishable by death.

To counter the apparent "crisis" threatening Germany, Hitler proposed a series of programs whereby the central government would take on all the power and political functions of the German states. The Enabling Act of 1933 gave the central government responsibility for all law enforcement and conferred on Hitler exclusive powers of decision making. This effectively transformed Hitler from chancellor to dictator. Hitler's promises that "the government will only make use of these powers insofar as they are essentially for carrying out vitally necessary measures" soon revealed themselves to be completely empty.

On November 7, 1938, a German Jewish refugee, Herschel Grynszpan, shot and killed a German official in Paris. It was the night of November 7 that became known as the "Night of Shattered Glass" or "Krystallnach," as the Nazi mobs rioted, destroying Jewish homes and synagogues and beating and killing the Jews themselves. Thereafter all opponents of the Nazis were merely branded as Jewish sympathizers and seen as criminals.

# Hollow Earth

According to some, it cannot be doubted that the Earth is in fact hollow and that there are people living inside, including descendants of survivors from the Atlantis culture. The outer crust being around one thousand miles thick, secret entrances are strategically placed around the Earth from which flying saucers emerge at regular intervals. In the middle of the hollow Earth is a central sun, smaller than our own sun, but large enough to give light and warmth. This explains the Aurora or the Midnight Sun in evidence near the poles, which are two popular sites for the Inner Earth doorways. With the central sun illuminating this inside world, it must be a tropical paradise, and possibly the setting for the story of the Garden of Eden. Humanity, it would seem, originated on the inside of the Earth and then moved to the outside.

There are numerous variations on the theory proposed above. Some would say that the flying saucers do indeed come from within the Earth, but that they are not the vessels of the descendants of Atlantis, or even the proof of alien life forms, but rather that they come from secret bases built by the Nazis who discovered an entrance into this secret world just before the collapse of the Third Reich. Apparently they are still hiding there and are waiting for an opportune moment to relaunch their campaign on the Outer Earth, having exterminated all the inner inhabitants who did not conform to their Aryan ideal. Others would have it that the inside of the Earth is inhabited, but the inhabitants are not physical in nature, so our normal earthly matter is no barrier to them. Or that the inhabitants are in fact four-dimensional beings, the extra dimension being incomprehensible but meaning that they are only able to communicate telepathically with us. Or that there are underground cities, but that were not built by any advanced human civilization, but rather by alien beings from other planets who use the center of the Earth as a base. Or even that the Earth is hollow, but that we are living on the inside, without realizing it. The real laws of physics could be completely different from what we believe.

The most pressing question of all is how we enter this hidden world. And that remains a mystery. Rumor would have it that the Earth is shaped like a giant doughnut, with two holes at each pole providing an entrance into the inner lands. Others would say that the only entrance is through old tunnels, caves and potholes. Evidence would also support the possibility of other hidden entrances to the inner realm in Area 51 and other mysterious regions of the world. However, what seems most likely of all is that any entrance to the center of the Earth will have been hidden from view with the use of advanced technology which would prevent detection at all, as some giant hole somewhere would not be able to be kept secret for very long, although, naturally, this could be what we are not meant to see in Area 51. This could be through the use of holograms, mind control or other psychological means, time travel, or methods not even imagined by our limited knowledge. One thing, however, seems definite. And that is that the inhabitants of this inner realm do not want to expose their identity to us because, assuming that they are aware of their situation, they surely would have done so by now.

And if they do not want us to know of their existence, it does not suggest that their motives are entirely amicable. Whether the government has proof of their existence or not cannot be proved, but a government that will not tell us what they do know about UFOs would certainly keep their origin a secret.

There are some who believe in the very real possibility of invasion and domination by the inhabitants of the center of the Earth. And it may well be that that is the origin of the Men in Black.

# Income Tax and
# Donald Duck

For years the U.S. had upheld the ideal of true democracy in funding their public services by means of a voluntary income tax. However, this democratic ideal only worked up to a point, as patriotism was not top on the list of most people's priorities. When it came to funding the war effort, only 11 percent of Americans were paying and it rapidly became clear that relying on people's patriotic goodwill was all very well in theory, but that the body and soul of the nation had to be kept together somehow if they were to win the war. In order to keep up the guise of a voluntary tax, Henry Morgenthau, the then Secretary of Treasury, contacted Walt Disney. Walt was told that the U.S. needed him to "help us sell people on paying the income tax."

This pricked at poor Walt's conscience a little because he inhabited a Disney world where justice always won out and he was distressed that this should even be an issue. As he saw it, failure to pay income tax was a capital offense and he wondered why the government didn't jail people who did not pay the income tax. However, the Internal Revenue Commissioner explained how they wanted to cultivate an attitude of patriotic goodwill and well-being among the people and retorted that "we want people to be enthusiastic about paying their taxes."

This satisfied Walt and he set about working on the film with renewed vigor. He had a six-week deadline to make a short film and to get it into the cinemas in February of 1943. Production on his other projects was suspended and a full-time work force labored night and day to produce the film. When the preliminary stages were completed, Walt headed back to Washington to preview them to Morgenthau.

The story was quite simple with obvious allegorical overtones. It started with Donald Duck, the very personification of patriotism, who was, however, reluctant to pay income taxes. The presentation continued with Donald being shown that paying the income tax would help win the war. With a whole new attitude, Donald quickly goes to work filling out his income tax return, becoming so enthusiastic about paying his tax that he races from California to Washington to submit his tax return in person.

Walt finished the film and it was released to cinemas for free. As a result, cinemas across the country canceled orders in favor of the Donald Duck cartoon.

The Treasury Department estimated that sixty million Americans saw the film and a Gallup Poll indicated that voluntary submission to the income tax increased by 37 percent.

# Irish Potato Famine

One hundred and fifty years ago, the Italian Mafia was trying to outdo its Irish rivals. During the mid-nineteenth century, they undertook an extensive plan to starve their chief rivals, the Irish crime bosses, out of their own home market. Rampaging up and down the length of Ireland in elaborate disguises, they ransacked farms and crops. Even they had little idea of quite how extensive the damage would be, and in this sense their plan worked. A massive emigration movement out of Ireland took place.

Unfortunately, however, the Italians failed to foresee the outcome of the famine, which resulted in an increased Irish presence in the "markets" of New York and Chicago eighty years later, where the Italians had previously done so well.

# Israeli Leader Assassination

Several years after the shooting of the Israeli Prime Minister Yitzhak Rabin at a peace rally in Tel Aviv, the details of the assassination are still not unearthed. But conspiracy theorists have prioritized the whole Rabin investigation, and the world has started to wonder if the suggestion of a government plot may have a more concrete foundation than mere speculation.

Two years after the death of Rabin, *Hatzofeh,* a right-wing newspaper, published a story highlighting a conspiracy theory being put forward on the Internet by a man named Uzi Barkan. At the same time, the government released previously unpublished findings of a commission that investigated the assassination. Government officials who have read the report say that the document reveals that an agent of the government security service, Shin Bet, urged the killer to shoot Rabin.

Once the document had been released, Netanyahu's government was demanding further investigations into the parts of the report that were as yet unavailable. It seemed that the most suspicious individual was a man called Avishai Raviv and he was immediately prosecuted. Raviv was a militant right-wing radical who was known for taking teenagers away to "summer camps" and then indoctrinating them with his political ideas. It would seem that Raviv had befriended Yigal Amir this way several years before, and then persuaded him to act as an assassin. He was the power behind the extremist right-wing group, Eyal, which was notorious for attracting political criminals, and it later transpired that he was paid by the government security service to provoke action amongst ultranationalists. Whether Raviv was or wasn't behind the crime, the fact that he knew Amir at all is suspicious and the fact that he may have acted as some kind of mentor to him in the past would suggest that his action is criminal in that he did nothing to stop Amir's plans once he was aware of his intentions to assassinate Rabin.

Investigations into the murder are being hampered by those government officials who claim that the inconsistencies surrounding the murder are nothing unusual and that it is almost impossible to find a crime where the facts are all clearly defined and laid-out. Moreover, a certain unwillingness to make the documents public because this would expose techniques of the intelligence service is a further obstacle. But this is what the public is after. Chemi Shalev, an Israeli political analyst, says that the suggestion that Shin Bet planned the murder is "outlandish . . . But the question of Raviv as an agent who somehow incited Amir, or whether the Shin Bet went too far in provoking incidents against the prime minister, that part of it is a question being asked by many people, even people on the left."

# JFK 1: Lee
Harvey Oswald

Thousands of conspiracy buffs believe that Lee Harvey Oswald was in fact put up to John F. Kennedy's assassination and then shot to stop him revealing the truth about what really happened. However, there is substantial evidence to suggest that Oswald *was* alone in shooting the president and that there was no conspiracy behind him.

If it was a conspiracy, it would have had to have been a more than superhumanly motivated team. For instance, how on earth could they have produced such a huge volume of evidence behind Oswald in such a short space of time? They would have only had a matter of days to make their plans after the announcement of the parade route and in that time, they would have had to approach an assassin, research their details and plant strategic evidence, all without being discovered.

Oswald's actions themselves were distinctly suspicious in the week prior to the assassination. Why should he have made a midweek trip to where the gun was stored, the day after he heard about JFK passing his workplace, when surely the conspirators would have been able to do so themselves? And why should he have left behind his wedding ring on the fateful day that JFK was shot? And why should he have left work early after the assassination and wandered around Dallas? Then, when approached by a police officer, why should he have shot him? All seems to point to the resounding evidence that Oswald was himself guilty.

If a conspiracy was at work, it would seem that it was not very well thought out. Why, if there was a conspiracy, should the assassination have taken place in such a public location? If an organization such as the CIA or the FBI was behind it, then surely they would have had access to a more sophisticated means of attack. And if it was a conspiracy, why choose Oswald in the first place? The CIA, FBI, Mafia or military-industrial complex would have had a plethora of expert gunmen to choose from. If a conspiracy of such mammoth proportions was being mounted, then hiring such an unprofessional assassin would have been an unusual and unlikely move. Unless, of course, this very unlikeliness was intended to serve as a bluff and cunning cover.

The Warren Commission came to the conclusion that Oswald was the lone assassin and their verdict was based on witness statements, detailed films, photographs, more information on the autopsy and access to highly classified documents which we simply do not have. Conspiracy buffs, however, would counter this outcome by arguing that the Warren Commission was influenced by the government.

# JFK 2: Anti-Green

The theory that the Kennedys were murdered by a bacterial conspiracy whose object it was to lower world oxygen levels cannot be ruled out. Atmospheric oxygen levels have steadily been falling since the Industrial Revolution. This may have been to our disadvantage, but the decrease has provided a paradise for non–oxygen breathing organisms, like the tetanus virus, which had been going extinct in prehistory as world oxygen levels rose. The coming of humanity and the subsequent reduction of atmospheric oxygen that was later complemented by deforestation and fossil-fuel burning gave a green light to bacteria. These organisms flourish in the industrial, oxygen-starved urban centers where most of the world's political power is concentrated. Who knows the extent of their power once they are in the right climate.

Kennedy was nothing if not radical and threatened to change this established order, to carry out a massive bacterial genocide. The microbial establishment perceived the powerful political figure as a threat. Indeed, such a figure could threaten their very existence. And so an assassination was arranged and carried out.

# JFK 3: Government Plot

There is the line of argument that the U.S. government killed JFK. And why? One proponent would have it that sixteen years after the Roswell incident, JFK wanted us to go extraterrestrial.

Conspiracy theorists state that the government had JFK assassinated in an effort to destroy the dream of space travel. Since the Roswell incident they had remained very mysterious about the truth of that day's events, thereby enjoying a measure of power over an unwittingly ignorant and vulnerable public. It follows, then, that the government would not be keen for society to learn the truth as a result of space travel, as whatever secret they had been harboring could finally be exposed.

# JFK 4: Fidel Castro

Fidel Castro, the Communist leader who took over Cuba, had previously shown much hostility towards the democratic United States.

When interrogated about the assassination, Castro denied any intention to assassinate the president, arguing that it would not be in his best interests at all, as such an action would provoke an American invasion against which he would have absolutely no chance of winning. Moreover, Kennedy himself had done very little to aggravate the Cuban leader. He had been very much against the idea of sending troops into Cuba, to the disgust of the military-industrial complex.

But even if he was not directly behind the assassination himself, it wouldn't have been hard for Fidel Castro or a colleague to investigate the background of Lee Harvey Oswald and persuade him to do it. Oswald was himself a Communist and had distributed wide propaganda supporting Cuba.

No one can know whether Castro would have wanted to do such a thing. He said that he was not unhappy with the current situation and he knew that the chances of Kennedy declaring war on him were unlikely. But having said that, others would have dearly loved to force him out of Cuba. The American oil barons were one of the many groups who wanted Fidel Castro out as he was destroying their factories and oil rigs in Cuba.

Kennedy had placed rigorous trade restrictions on the oil barons, thereby costing them millions, and with no attention being paid to this in the public sphere and no solution in sight, could they have taken the matter into their own hands?

The relations between Fidel Castro, Kennedy, the oil barons and Oswald are murky to say the least. But we do know for sure that there was considerable unresolved malaise. Could this have provoked one of the parties to murder?

# JFK 5: Mafia

It is a little known fact that Kennedy's brother Robert was working to reduce the organized crime gangs of America including the Mafia. All the Mafia gang members had said that it would be beneficial to them if either Robert or John were out of the picture.

One could, of course, see the assassination as a severe warning to the U.S. government to cut short their inquiries into the world of crime there and then. An assassination would certainly have been a dramatic way of proving to the world that no one, not even the president, could dare to tamper with them.

Witnesses claimed that they had seen Oswald on several occasions with Mafia gang members. And if Oswald had been working for the Mafia, could Jack Ruby have been employed to assassinate him in turn to keep him from revealing the truth? Oswald had hinted that he knew more than he was telling.

The Mafia's intentions were not peaceable. Constantly issuing demands for more weapons and men, they had been outraged when Kennedy had been threatening to pull out of Vietnam, so an assassination would have been an effective solution. When Kennedy was assassinated, the paper which he had drawn up stating that he was considering pulling out of Vietnam was apparently lost.

Could the Mafia have infiltrated the American government? Could some of its members have been bribed to influence the proceedings in which the Mafia were interested? Could this be the reason why there was never a full investigation into the possibility of a conspiracy?

# JFK 6: CIA

Kennedy and the CIA had reached an impasse over the Cuba situation. Neither was prepared to give. Kennedy blamed the CIA and the CIA blamed Kennedy, accusing him of not having given them enough resources to work with. There certainly was a great deal of hostility in the air and even if the assassination was a more dramatic remedy than had been initially intended, it could have been that Kennedy had discovered a plot against either him personally or the government. Could it be that he needed to be silenced before he could say anything? Certainly one cannot rule out the possibility that the assassination was an act of self-defense, covering the intentions of the CIA. If it was to work, it would be essential to leave no trace behind.

And in this situation, it would have been imperative to use an outside assassin. They could easily have put a threat on Kennedy's head, Oswald could have heard all about it and then carried out the CIA's dirty work for them. The CIA would have had the personnel and expertise to cover their tracks, and the very unprofessional nature of Oswald could itself have been a double bluff.

Moreover, the CIA could have used one of their secret

service agents. Oswald could have been no more than the gunman that the public was meant to see. There are reports of agents on the scene that were not meant to exist. The theory of the second gunman could easily have been true. If so, could there have been an expert gunman hiding in the grassy knoll?

# JFK 7: Military-Industrial Complex

Kennedy's plans to pull out of Vietnam certainly created much dissatisfaction, not only among the Mafia who thrive on war, but also the military-industrial complex who were already angry over his handling of Cuba.

Kennedy's reelection was all but certain and he had already issued a statement saying that once the elections were over he would pull his troops out of Vietnam. Yet just four days after the assassination, Johnson sent in more troops, totally going against Kennedy's wishes but delighting the Mafia and even more so, the military-industrial complex.

The question of whether Kennedy could have angered the military-industrial complex enough for them to order his assassination is unresolved, but they were certainly unimpressed by his actions.

The other question is where the FBI comes into it all. They wouldn't be considered as the assassins, only as conspirators. It seems unlikely that they would consider such an overt action, as they tend to go for more secretive and less publicly orientated tasks.

But even if they were not directly responsible for the assassination, the FBI is responsible for the country's welfare, so it is possible that it would have had some prior intelligence of the assassination.

# JFK 8: The KGB

Right-wing conspiracy theorists would have Oswald perform the deed single-handedly all in the name of the Communist cause. Spending two years in Russia, Leonochoff, as he was then known, married the daughter of one of the Russian Intelligentsia and was indoctrinated to the benefits of the Communist way of life. Moreover, the Cold War was at its most lethal and when it came to it, Leonochoff was quite happy to do the honors, all in the name of love.

Professor Revilo Oliver wrote an account taking up 123 pages in the Warren Report, and claims that the international Communist conspiracy killed Kennedy because he was not serving it as efficiently as he had promised. Kennedy showed no signs of delivering America to Communism. Oliver also concluded mournfully that while Kennedy, a Communist tool, was the object of national grief, not a tear was shed over the end of Adolf Hitler.

# King James I
# of England

Despite constant attacks by wealthy Catholic nations, England was holding her own in the Tudor age and was in fact fast establishing herself as a leading Western nation, both culturally and militarily. Even the Spanish Armada posed no threat of domination and the reign of Elizabeth I was one of prosperity and security.

However, once Elizabeth died, there was no obvious successor to the throne and the country was thrown into some confusion. This gave England's enemies the perfect opportunity to attack. And they were quick to seize the opportunity. Three of England's Catholic enemies got together and hatched a plot. By placing the King of Scotland on the English throne, they believed that the reign of the Scottish ruler contrasting with the vastly different English system would result in such disaster that civil war would be inevitable. At this stage the Irish would revolt, driving the English out of Ireland. Next the Catholic nations would unite and send a gigantic army to conquer England and restore the Pope as the supreme religious authority. The Scottish monarch was considered quite dispensable. This plot very nearly came to fruition, with civil war resulting, not in the reign of James I, but that of his son Charles I.

This time delay only made for complacency among the Catholic nations and when civil war did erupt and they had the perfect opportunity to attack, the necessary concentration of troops had not been brought together. This meant that Oliver Cromwell, the Puritan leader, came down and the English crown was restored. Without support from the other nations, the Irish just did not have the strength to expel England from Ireland and the English people only hardened their resolve to remain Protestant in defiance of their Catholic opponents.

# Kursk Nuclear Submarine

The *Kursk* nuclear submarine disaster, in which 118 people died, was an event widely covered by the world's media in late summer 2000, but most of the coverage of this tragedy focused on the unsuccessful rescue attempt and on the personal stories of the submariners trapped under the Barents Sea, encased in a metal tomb. But was the disaster a simple naval accident or was there a more sinister explanation for what happened 60 feet below freezing Russian waters?

The five-year-old double-hulled Oscar II-class submarine was part of a fifty-strong fleet of warships involved in Russian naval exercises off Russia's northern coastline. But it was two large explosions on board that triggered disaster for the crew. The cause of those explosions remains highly contentious, however. Theories include a collision with the seabed, with a British or American submarine straying into Russian territorial waters, an icebreaker or cargo ship, an old World War II mine, or an act of deliberate sabotage. It was claimed by Dmytro Korchynskyy, head of the nationalist Ukrainian Political Association, that the *Kursk* was targeted by Chechen separatists. He also claimed that the Russian security services had been warned about this two weeks before but had not taken the threat seriously.

But it may be that the true cause lies outside of Russia altogether. Despite the end of the Cold War, British and American submarines have continued to play cat-and-mouse games with their Russian counterparts under the Atlantic Ocean. Naval crews on rival submarines often shadow each other's movements in these "games," but sometimes collisions can occur, with eleven occurrences since 1967 in the Barents Sea alone. Anonymous sources from inside the Ministry of Defense say that a British submarine may have been involved but even if this were true the British government would never admit to it publicly. Intriguingly, on the day of the disaster the Russian national press agency, Interfax, reported that unidentified military sources had said that an object resembling part of a "foreign submarine tower" had been discovered 330 meters from the *Kursk* on the seabed. The same sources said the most likely explanation for the sinking was collision with another submarine, "most likely British." However, this was vehemently denied by both the British and Russian defense ministries.

Senior Russian naval officers have their own version of what happened. They also believe a collision was the source of the disaster, but with an American submarine. They claim that two American submarines were conducting spy operations, and have produced satellite photographs of an American submarine docked in the Norwegian naval base of Bergen, at a time just after the *Kursk* sank. The Russian navy insist this proves the submarine had surfaced for repairs resulting from the impact. Submarines are designed specifically to spend long periods underwater without the need to dock for supplies, proving, as the Russians see it, the case that it had docked for repairs. In addition, photographs were taken during the failed rescue mission showing damage to the body of the craft consistent with theories of a scraping collision. The Americans deny these allegations but, intriguingly, do admit to conducting operations in the area at the time of the disaster.

The most tantalizing explanation, though, is that one of the torpedoes on board the *Kursk* dramatically exploded, causing the devastating blast that was detected as far away as Alaska, and measured 4.2 on the Richter scale. Theories abound that a top secret ultra high-speed torpedo named Skhval was being covertly tested, a torpedo said to outperform any torpedo in the NATO arsenal, claims which would heighten Russian secrecy concerns and for American spying operations.

Contradictory claims have also emerged with the release of secret British government documents involving a submarine accident off the English coastline in 1955. This involved the use of high test peroxide to supply the torpedo's engine which is thought to have caused an explosion. It was this danger which led to the technology being disbanded by the British but, perplexingly, may have continued to be used by Russia and have been the major contributor to the *Kursk* tragedy.

The Communist newspaper *Komsomolskaya Pravda* in 2001 suggested a cover-up by the Russian admiralty. It claimed a message was sent from the submarine to land-based commanders before the blast, saying, "We have a malfunctioning torpedo. Request permission to fire it." By denying this version, the Russian authorities conveniently detach blame from themselves, and from President Vladimir Putin, who was criticized for not cutting short his holiday during the crisis. To add to this sense of connivance, when the *Kursk* was raised from the seabed the Russian government said it believed that it was far too dangerous to raise the torpedo compartment with it, which contained live warheads and had to be separated to aid the lifting procedure. This averted any potential criticism of what may have been found in the torpedo chambers, thus saving the reputation of Russia's embattled armed forces.

With these varying interpretations of what took place,

the only consensus that has emerged is in the secrecy shown by all sides alleged to have been involved, and the nonemergence of any widely accepted explanation. It is this sense of official denial and hint of cover-up which generates the overwhelming feelings of injustice felt by the families of those involved.

# Kurt Cobain

One of the most intriguing current conspiracy theories is that surrounding the premature and sudden death of world-famous singer Kurt Cobain. The truth seems more than slightly elusive. Questions of whether it really was a suicide are closely tied with the issues of whether his allegedly estranged wife, Courtney Love, was involved in any conspiracy. The further one delves into the mystery, the fewer ends seem to tie up.

What seems strangest of all is the suicide note left by Cobain directly prior to his dramatic exit scene, given that the tone really was not suicidal, with statements such as "I have it good, very good, and I'm grateful." The entire note was written in the present tense and seems to be a far cry from the final words of a man about to kill himself.

According to psychologists at the rehabilitation center Cobain had visited only the week before, as well as close friends, no one had suspected that he was suicidal, which in the light of his Rome "suicide attempt" a few months earlier seems suspicious. Kurt had written Courtney a note after that incident which included one line which she said was "very definitely suicidal." "Dr. Baker says I would have to choose between life and death," Kurt had written. "I'm choosing death."

There is the theory that Cobain was quite simply terrified for his life after walking out on a $9.5 million contract to headline Lollapalooza and that this inspired him to commit suicide. And the fact that the shotgun was loaded with three shells when the fatal deed was done could have been part of a plan to make his suicide look like murder.

Strangest of all, police failed to find any fingerprints at all on the gun. Of course, perhaps Kurt had carefully covered his traces and wiped the gun down, but such behavior is not what one expects from someone on the verge of suicide, and in any case, if it really was suicide, why the need for the big cover-up?

It is not to be denied that murdering the father of your child is fairly uncommon and the fact that Courtney and Kurt were not getting on well before his death would seem little justification for cold-blooded killing. However, she could have had several other possible motives. In January 1994 Cobain told *Rolling Stone* that he might well be divorcing Courtney. Apparently divorce papers had already been drawn up by the time of his death. And shortly before the death itself, Courtney had apparently instructed one of her lawyers to get the "meanest, most vicious divorce lawyer" she could find. Kurt had also hinted that he wanted Courtney taken out of his will, in which case she would have gained a lot more financially from a suicide before the will could be changed than from a divorce. If Kurt were to die, sales for Kurt's band Nirvana would rocket. And Courtney would benefit financially.

The official line is that Kurt committed suicide. In the days and weeks following his death, fans began killing themselves in empathy with their fallen hero. In light of this suicide rush, the backlash would be devastating if police reversed their original judgment and opened a murder investigation.

# Lennon's Assassination

John Lennon was shot on December 8, 1980 outside the Dakota in New York by Mark David Chapman, aged twenty-five. Was Chapman merely another disturbed killer, unsure of his own motives, or could there in fact have been political reasons behind the killings?

It would seem unlikely that Chapman had killed Lennon to be famous. During his life, he turned down thirty to forty interviews, and said himself, "I am not a seeker after publicity." He never allowed documentaries to be filmed with him and never gave an interview. Moreover, his composure after he had shot Lennon was quite remarkable.

Lennon was one of the most politically active rock stars of his generation. This, coupled with his reputation as a drug user, classified him as an undesirable in the eyes of the authorities, making it difficult for him to obtain a green card to come and live in the U.S. The coinciding of his return to his former greatness with Reagan's rise to power is interesting to say the least. Reagan's policies were radical and Lennon was the only person who would

have been able to bring out millions of people to protest.
The question therefore has to be asked whether there
may have been some kind of political involvement in his
murder.

# Lockerbie

In February 2004, Libya delivered a letter to the UN Security Council stating that it "accepts responsibility for the actions of its officials" with regards to this horrific air disaster. Nevertheless, this has failed to quiet controversy and suspicion over the explanation for the events of that fateful day.

The 1988 bombing of Pan Am 103 over Lockerbie cost 270 lives and was one of the most catastrophic "accidents" of the twentieth century. Fingers were initially pointed at Iran and Syria, who were allies of the Ahmed Jibril faction. However, then U.S. President George Bush Senior needed help and sponsorship in his war effort against Iraq, and the blame was shifted accordingly. An angry Bush threatened to attack Libya if it failed to come up with two of its "intelligence agents" who had supposedly planted the bomb on an Air Malta plane that connected with Pan Am 103. At that time, Libya denied the accusation and refused to cooperate.

The English *Independent* newspaper completely negated that line of inquiry, and testified that a recently discovered internal FBI memo found "no concrete indication that any piece of luggage was unloaded from Air Malta 180 . . . then [placed] on board Pan Am 103." This came after other sources which had reported that the Iranians were responsible for commissioning the bombings.

But was there really a cover-up? Certainly the *Guardian* claimed that "a secret deal between Germany and Iran is reported to have led to the release of a prominent suspect in the Lockerbie bombing." We do know that the suspect, Abdel Ghadanfar, was arrested two months before the bombing for terrorist activities producing similar devices to that used on Pan Am 103. His release in November 1994 was carried out in utmost secrecy, leading to further outrage on the part of victims' families who, understandably, are looking to be presented with a definite culprit.

# LSD Research

The CIA's interest in how the drug LSD alters normal behavior patterns has been condemned as "morally and legally unacceptable." Some one thousand five hundred U.S. soldiers were victims of drug experimentation. Some claimed that they had agreed to become guinea pigs only through pressure from their superior officers. Many claimed to have suffered from severe depression and psychological stress as a result.

One such soldier was Master Sergeant Jim Stanley. LSD was put in his drinking water and he claims the process destroyed him psychologically. His hallucinations continued even after he returned to his normal duties. His service record suffered, as did his marriage—he began beating his wife and children. It was not until seventeen years later that he was informed by the military that he had been used as an LSD experiment. He sued the government, but the Supreme Court ruled that no soldier could sue the Army for LSD experiments—a controversial outcome for many, who protest that experimentation with unknowing human subjects is an infringement of the most basic human liberty.

# Lunarians

Most people have heard about the mythical Man in the Moon. But suppose that he is not really a myth? Suppose that there may in fact be more than one man? Rumor has it that hundreds, possibly thousands of people make up a mysterious lunar society, one that is technologically superior to even the most advanced secret societies on Earth. The details of the society are sketchy, but what facts we do have involve both Sigmund Freud and the CIA, two of the more mysterious entities in world history.

The Sigmund Freud we knew and loved was a member of the aforementioned society in which everyone is a clone of each other, so, in fact, we are dealing with a race of mini-Freuds. Freud's conscience began to prick him when he arrived at the startling realization that his fellow Lunarians might well use their psychological and scientific superiority to take over the weaker Earth-bound culture. So he secretly traveled down to Earth, and imparted bits and pieces of Lunarian knowledge which are what most people attribute to be his psychology.

Although Freud never fully completed what he had set out to do and never gave his true identity away, his fellow clones started to feel threatened. Eventually they decided to follow in Freud's footsteps, but instead of continuing with the psychologist's philanthropic intentions in aiming to enlighten the Earth's entire population, they targeted those in positions of power in the hope that they would act as enforcers of Lunarian rule. Freud's fears were justly founded. The Lunarians were planning to take over the Earth.

We don't know how, why or when the Lunarians first made contact with the U.S. authorities. But we do know that it was around the same time that the Central Intelligence Agency Group (CIG) was formed. This was replaced by the CIA in 1947. It all seems rather more than purely coincidental. It seems quite without doubt that in setting up the CIA, an organization was established comprising entirely of Lunarians. Lunarians have infiltrated other sectors of the American government and now hold high positions of state as well as in the army and the navy.

Of course, opponents to the theory will point out that man has traveled to the moon and has sent many robot probes to carry out extensive research. But it would have been quite simple for the Lunarians to have intercepted the robot probes and given them false data. And suppose the astronauts were brainwashed with the same information that had been fed to the robot probes? The Lunarians would have had plenty of time to see us coming. The moon is plenty big enough to provide temporary hiding places.

The big question is what the Lunarians' next step will be. Once they have infiltrated all the media organizations, world domination will not be far away. Perhaps we should have listened harder to Freud.

# Malcolm X

On February 21, 1965, Malcolm X was killed by a shotgun blast at close range as he began a speech at the Audubon Ballroom in New York. On March 10, 1966, three men were convicted of murder in the first degree. One, Talmadge Hayer, a member of the Nation of Islam, confessed he was one of the gunmen, but insisted that the other two, Thomas 15X Johnson and Norman 3X Butler, were innocent.

The general feeling was that the Nation was behind the killing because Elijah Muhammad, the Nation's leader, had made it publicly known that he resented Malcolm's defection from the Nation and feared that he would reveal Nation secrets. One damaging secret was the allegation that the Nation had met with the American Nazi Party and the Ku Klux Klan and accepted money from racist whites—all of whom agreed with the Nation's policy of racial separation. Another secret was that Elijah Muhammad had fathered numerous "divine babies" with half a dozen teenaged Nation secretaries.

There are other theories about the assassination, too. One is that a narcotics cartel, perhaps Chinese, ordered the murder because of Malcolm's fight against Harlem's drug trade. Another theory implicates the CIA and FBI in the killing. Malcolm was in the process of embarrassing the country by accusing the U.S. of racism and human rights violations in Third World countries. A variation of this theory is that the government had Malcolm killed because he was moving away from racial separatism and on the verge of becoming an effective civil rights leader.

The real reasons behind Malcolm's assassination will probably never be known. His killing, like that of John F. Kennedy, will continue to be a source of conjecture for years to come.

# Man on the Moon

E ven for those of us with no direct memories of the monumental moon landings, questions exist about the manned trip to the moon. Did people from Earth actually travel to the moon? Those who witnessed Neil Armstrong's landing on the moon wondered at the time if something fishy was going on, if in fact the event ever really happened, if the entire thing was a cover-up presented by NASA, filmed using cinematic tricks.

Questions became more pressing with the release of the film *Capricorn One,* produced by Warner Brothers in 1978, which went so far as to record on screen how some of the effects might have been accomplished. This showed a trip to Mars, cleverly faked so that the public believed what was happening. But people started to wonder whether this was no more than a representation of what had happened with the moon shots of the late '60s and early '70s.

In reality the possibility of a conspiracy is probably unlikely. In the technological climate as it then was, it would, ironically, have been easier to send a man to the moon and film him there than to attempt to reproduce the moon's environment on Earth. Even more modern films like *Apollo 13* had considerable difficulties in simulating weightlessness for shots of up to twenty seconds. The lengthy film material that was returned from the moon cannot easily be explained if it was a fake.

It would have been no mean feat to fake the launch of the enormous rocket craft, *Saturn V,* and again, it would seem to be far easier to go ahead and complete the project than to perform a massive illusion and somehow con the hundreds of thousands who were watching that the rocket took off into space when actually it did no such thing.

But this does not mean that everything we receive from NASA is exactly as it is portrayed. Even if man did travel to the moon, did they find objects and structures that were never revealed to the public? Did they travel with ulterior motives? These theories are harder to disprove, and to know that we are only receiving information as it is filtered through the NASA censors is disquieting to say the least.

# Marilyn Monroe

Of the hundreds of books that have been published about Marilyn Monroe since she died, fifty are full-length accounts of only the last week of her life and the multiple conspiracy theories that have grown up around her premature death. The bottom line was that Marilyn committed suicide, but even if she did kill herself by the overdose of hoarded Nembutal barbiturates, this verdict does not rule out the fact that there was a large number of people who wanted to be rid of her for one reason or another. If her death was a suicide, it was undoubtedly a very well timed suicide.

Marilyn's affairs with highly placed individuals could have allowed her direct access to some of the innermost state secrets of the U.S. The CIA would be an obvious suspect in her questionable death if this was the case. The Mafia also come into question if rumors are true that she knew too much about a possible relationship between the Mafia and Frank Sinatra; other theorists claim that the Kennedys somehow killed Marilyn before she could make her long-standing affair with John known to the public. There are also many who believe that her carers in her final weeks killed her for her riches.

And, furthermore, Marilyn could have been killed by aliens who were trying to cover up the fact that JFK was a member of a global unit of Freemasons bent on world domination through the ancient science of black magic.

# Mars

Even if life no longer exists on Mars, it would seem more and more indisputable that some degree of life has once existed there. After Earth, Mars is the most habitable planet in our solar system, and, despite now having freezing temperatures of around minus 50 degrees, research has shown that once upon a time, the planet enjoyed a similar climate to our own. Studies suggest that all chances of inhabiting Mars were destroyed by a massive onslaught of comets and/or asteroids. The planet's surface is covered with craters as a testimony to this.

But recently photographs of possible microscopic fossils of bacterialike organisms found in Martian meteorites have been unveiled. Life must have, at one time, existed. And, while, at this stage we are not talking about little green men, startling evidence has shown that intelligent life almost definitely set foot on Mars at some stage in the past. Photographs of remarkable pyramid structures have come back from the planet, structures that seem not only to be artificially constructed, but, moreover, bear a similar "face" to that of the Great Sphinx at Giza. The implications of this are quite staggering.

If the pyramids on Mars are what they seem to be, it would seem quite certain that they bear some link to the ones on Earth. But if they do, then there must be a totally radical rethinking of our whole civilization. Presumably, if there is a link, we can only surmise that an ancient, far superior civilization to our own went to Mars and built the pyramids. Or else, perhaps even more disturbingly, that an ancient civilization came over from Mars and, in turn, built the pyramids here. Neither can we rule out the possibility that the pyramids were actually created by a civilization whose roots we cannot hope to understand, coming from outside our solar system, a civilization that came into our galaxy and left the pyramids as their trademark.

But what could the builders of these mysterious monuments have been trying to say? What silent message are we witness to as we regard the vast testimony to a past generation? Are the pyramids merely the proof of a prehistory so ancient that our minds cannot comprehend it, or could they be spelling out some kind of warning? And if they have come from a civilization beyond our own solar system, it is possible that the threat they pose may be imminent.

A popular question raised by conspiracy theorists is whether or not investigations on our Earth were carried out in a similar way to our investigations on Mars. In the long term, scientists have plans for a series of experiments whereby, by means of the transportation of simple bacteria onto Mars, life could be introduced onto the planet. Nobody can disprove the theory that life on Earth was started in the same way. A more advanced and older civilization than our own could have deliberately manufactured the way we live. If this was the case, further questions are prompted regarding the Martians' purpose or fate for us. Are we, for example, the playthings of some mammoth intergalactic conspiracy?

Theorists also voice concerns that there are a select few here on Earth who know more than they are willing to share. The *Mars Observer,* sent out in 1993, mysteriously vanished as it neared to within three days of the planet. To a cynical mind, this is very convenient—what better means of covering up what it found if NASA didn't like it? The *Observer* could have been sent into orbit three days earlier than the world was told, giving officials time to digest the information it discovered. If this turned out to be disturbing evidence of alien life, a claim that the probe had disappeared would effectively curb public malaise.

There have, nevertheless, been successful attempts to land probes on Mars, including the *Mars Express* and *Spirit*. However, these have been plagued with communication problems, meaning that little or no information could be relayed to ground controllers. There are schools of thought suggesting that the eventual pictures portrayed in the media are nothing but an Earthly fabrication, or, more worrying still, that the Martians have taken the explorers and are sending back only the images they want us to see.

# Mars Life

．

Afraid of international panic, it would seem that NASA and the American government are withholding pictures that show life on Mars. However, a picture indicating that life on Mars exists, or previously existed, is in circulation. It shows a fossilized skeleton of a small humanoid creature near the *Sojourner* space buggy. The United States government refuses to acknowledge the skeleton. End of story.

# Martin Luther King, Jr.

James Earl Ray confessed to the assassination of Martin Luther King, Jr. on being arrested in England where he was tracked after police found his fingerprint on a rifle recovered near the scene. Suspicions of conspiracy in the assassination immediately arose because of the improbable circumstances surrounding Ray. How could a blatantly petty and inexperienced thief (his criminal career was typified by such offences as taxicab holdups and small corner-shop robberies, for which he usually got caught) pull off a complicated crime such as a celebrity assassination and make his way to London via Atlanta, Toronto and Portugal? How could he afford the travel expenses, much less plan the convoluted escape in advance? Congressional investigators estimated that Ray spent at least $9,607 between his prison escape and his London arrest, an amount roughly equal to $38,000 by current values. And how could he concoct such an elaborate scheme, yet still be careless enough to leave the murder weapon at the scene of the crime with his fingerprint on it?

Days before he pleaded guilty, Ray expressed misgivings in a letter to his lawyer, Percy Foreman: "On this guilty plea, it seems to me that I am taking all the blame, which is all right with me." In another passage, Ray said, "It was my stupidity which got me into this." Memphis plastic surgeon Dr. McCarthy DeMere, who served as Ray's physician at the jail, testified before Congress in 1978 that he once asked Ray. "Did you really do it?" "Well, let's put it this way: I wasn't in it by myself," and that's all he would say to me," DeMere testified before Congress in 1978. Ray recounted his guilty plea just days after he entered it, saying that he had been talked into committing the crime. He was set up, he said, by a mystery man named "Raoul," who had recruited Ray into a smuggling enterprise.

Early in 1996 a woman named Glenda Grabow came forward saying she had been carrying a secret for years. She knew Raoul. Her claim is detailed in a book by Dr. William F. Pepper, who tracked the man and said the elusive Raoul now lives somewhere in the Northeast. But he is originally from Portugal, one of Ray's destinations on his travels between the assassination and his capture. "Raoul" was a weapons smuggler, said Grabow, and she claims to have seen him off-loading and assembling illegal guns. Ray has said that he ran guns into Canada and Mexico for Raoul.

# Men in Black

**M**en in Black have become a myth. And a terrifying one at that. Usually connected to UFO activity, the MIB seem to have developed a pattern whereby they will appear after any kind of extraterrestrial encounter and terrorize those unfortunate enough to have had such an encounter in the first place. The archetypal Men in Black are given away by the trademark of their black suits, and tend to travel in pairs in black cars, although they have been known to use the infamous black helicopter. Witnesses claim that they often look foreign, are abnormally tall and sometimes have no fingernails. Their spoken English is frequently labored and spoken in an indistinguishable accent, seemingly without having to move their lips.

Jenny Randles records in her book *Investigating the Truth Behind the MIB* multiple cases of MIB activity. The case of Shirley Greenfield, for example, victim of an alien abduction, is explored in the light of the MIB visitation that occurred shortly afterwards. According to Randles, nine days after the abduction two men appeared at the Greenfields' home demanding to speak to Shirley and threatening to return later if they were denied entrance.

The men apparently held a curious power over the Green-fields and displayed distinctly eccentric behavior. Not addressing each other by name, they simply called each other "Commander" and refused to say where they were from, simply refuting Mr. Greenfield's assumptions that they were journalists. While they were talking, they appeared to be tape-recording the conversation using a square-shaped box, but one that was totally opaque, with no microphone, and one whose tape did not need to be changed at any point during the proceedings. Randles goes on to show how they grilled Shirley aggressively about her abduction and issued her with a strict warning at the end of the conversation that she must not relay it to anyone. Wheedling everything that had happened out of her, the only thing that Shirley seemed reluctant to tell them was about the physical marks that the abduction had left on her upper arms. However, over the course of the next week, Shirley was plagued by telephone calls from the "Commander," persistently asking her about physical evidence of what had happened. When Shirley finally confessed that yes, she did have physical marks to prove what had happened, the interrogator seemed relieved and the telephone calls stopped.

The big question regarding the MIB is who are they? Are they a part of a government conspiracy to silence the victims of UFO activity? Is there an extra dimension that such activity has unearthed but one that the government is anxious not to reveal? Could this be a manifestation of the government's conspiracy with an extraterrestrial race, a conspiracy involving human abduction for medical experiment in exchange for technological know-how? Or is the mystery of the MIB more frightening still, and could they be from a power or a force of which we are completely unaware? One thing seems certain: they are prepared to go to any lengths to keep their identity undercover. One can well ask what their motives are in doing this, and it would seem that if there were a logical, rational explanation, it would be out in the open.

# Microchip Implants: The Mark of the Beast?

At a time when the new "chip and PIN" method of payment is being implemented throughout the UK with officials stating that "the majority of cardholders will have a chip and PIN card by the end of 2004," a worried few are voicing concerns over an imminent apocalypse.

It is not such a great leap to an age much represented in Hollywood when we will no longer have to bother with PINs, checkbooks or passports. Everything about us will be stored in a chip the size of a grain of rice, embedded in our right hands, where it can be read or traced through walls and great distances. Just such an implantable biometric chip, capable of tracking a person for the rest of his or her life, was named Best in Show at the 2003 International Science Exhibitors show. There are obvious benefits to a chip system—but will we be prepared to accept this loss of privacy?

Some religious groups are warning that loss of privacy is the least of our troubles. Quoting the Bible, they warn that if society follows this invasive route, it will be an ominous fulfilment of a prophecy made a long time ago:

*And he causeth all, both small and great, rich and poor,*
*free and bond, to receive a mark in their right hand, or*
*in their foreheads: And that no man might buy or sell,*
*save he that had the mark, or the name of the beast, or*
*the number of his name. Here is wisdom. Let him that*
*hath understanding count the number of the beast: for it*
*is the number of a man; and his number is 666. (Reve-*
*lations 13:16–18)*

According to Tim Willard, managing director of the U.S. magazine *Futurists,* everyone's Social Security number will consist of "a new, global, eighteen-digit mesh-block config-uration of international numbers that will allow people to be tracked internationally." Willard goes on to predict that this number will take the form of three sets of six—6-6-6.

A further branch of this theory forecasts that there will be a single world government, divided into ten nations. One of these nations—the European Union—is already formed and developing, with a single currency, which re-cently came into play in most of its participating countries. If we reject this "mark" it is thought that we will have no place in a soon-to-be-established new society. On the other hand, its implementation could spell the coming of Judg-ment Day.

# Mind Control

A short media report in July 1995, in the immediate aftermath of a heat wave, told of the deaths of three inmates of Vacaville Medical Facility who had been imprisoned in non–air conditioned cells. Two of these inmates, the report went on, may have died as the result of medical treatment. No official inquiries were made.

But what was the medical treatment that may have caused their deaths? The Medical Facility suggests that they may well have been the result of mind-control tests.

Those subject to the mind-control experiments would often be prisoners for completely random, often petty crimes. They would be given indefinite sentences, freedom being dependent on how well the experiments went. One individual, for example, arrested for joy-riding and given a two year sentence, was subject to experiments and, yielding useful results, was held for eighteen years.

Here are just a few of the experiments used by governments in mind-control research:

- A naked inmate is strapped to a board. His wrists and ankles are handcuffed to the board. His head is fixed rigidly in place. He is left in a pitch-black cell, unable to perform the most basic bodily functions.

When a meal is delivered only one of his hands is unstrapped so that he can feel around in the dark for his food and attempt to pour liquid into his mouth without being able to lift his head.

• One drug used for experimentation creates a muscle relaxant so strong that within thirty seconds paralysis begins to set in, causing the heart to slow down to sixty beats a minute and the respiratory system to spasm.

• Another drug induces uncontrollable vomiting that lasts from fifteen minutes to an hour.

• Another creates severe body rigidity, restlessness, blurred vision, acute muscular pain and uncontrollable trembling.

Perhaps it is not altogether surprising that the Department of Health, Education and Welfare and the U.S. government would rather keep these experiments hushed, especially given their similarity to medical experiments carried out in Nazi concentration camps.

# Mozart's Death

"**M**ozart is dead.... Because his body swelled up after death, some people believe that he was poisoned.... Now that he is dead the Viennese will at last realize what they had lost in him."

So ran a report from a Prague correspondent in a Berlin newspaper less than a month after Wolfgang Amadeus Mozart's death. Conspiracy theories were mooted immediately. Questions of who had killed possibly the greatest musician ever to have lived have intrigued historians over the years attempting to unravel the threads of the mystery surrounding such a premature death.

One theory is that Antonio Salieri, the long-time arch rival of Mozart, killed him. Indeed, towards the end of his own life, Salieri seems to have lost his reason and attempted suicide. From that moment until his own death, rumor had it that he had in fact confessed to the murder of Mozart. However, what could Salieri actually have gained from Mozart's death? Although Mozart was by far the superior composer of the two, in material terms Salieri actually had the better paid job as Imperial Kappellmeister, a post which, no doubt, Mozart would have dearly loved.

Not only did he have a better salary, but also more oppor-
tunities for creativity in terms of having the freedom to
compose, and at the time Salieri's operas had at least as
fine a reputation as Mozart's. Materially, it would seem
that Mozart should have had a stronger urge to kill Salieri.
As the film *Amadeus* would have it, Salieri's wrath against
his rival could have been inspired purely out of jealousy that
while he toiled away laboriously to produce his art, which
was, in the end, no more than second-rate, Mozart worked
apparently effortlessly, achieving what was quite indis-
putably the work of genius.

Others would point the finger at the Freemasons, with
whom Mozart had become involved in his youth. *Die
Zauberflote* is essentially a Masonic opera, and shows the
artist's struggle against Christianity, and in particular
the Catholic Church. But at the same time, the Masonic
content of the opera is constantly put to question. Mozart
did not take Masonic word as law. He came from an un-
questionably Christian tradition and moreover, a Christian
chorale may be heard in the duet of the armed men in the
opera. Sarastro, the archetypal Masonic figure, is not good
through and through and appears as a kidnapper. Apparently
Mozart had planned to establish a new order, rival to the
Freemasons, going by the name of "Die Grotte," suggesting that his relationship with the Masons themselves was
not entirely happy. Apparently he had taken his clarinettist
friend (and sometime Mason) Anton Stadler into his confidence and had consequently been betrayed by him. As a final possible point of evidence, it would seem strange that
the Masons made no financial contribution towards his
funeral expenses and were prepared to let Mozart be buried
in a pauper's grave.

# Nazca Lines

The Nazca Lines have been a perpetual source of fascination for travelers for centuries. The lines appear in the Nazca desert on a high plateau in the Peruvian Andes, 250 miles south of Lima. The thousands of lines resemble drawings of birds, spiders, lizards, apes, fish and other unidentifiable animals, as well as simple geometric patterns, shapes and straight lines. Many of the drawings are indistinguishable on the ground and can only be appreciated from the air. As the ancient Nazca Indians had no known method of flying it is unclear how or why they created them. Carbon dating technology has estimated they are at least one thousand five hundred years old.

Various researchers have attempted to explain these mysterious patterns throughout the ages. Many explanations make connections with outer space. Paul Kosok, an American scholar, tried to find alignments between the drawings and the stars to create an astronomical connection. It is believed that the Nazca Indians may have created the drawings as a form of worship to the gods, possibly linked to the natural world or to the success of their harvests.

Others believe the depictions weren't created by the

Indians at all, that it was visiting aliens who constructed them. Erich von Daniken published a book in 1968 entitled *Chariot of the Gods?*, where he put forward the theory that the lines represented a landing strip for alien spaceships. Von Daniken thought these extraterrestrials also constructed other wonders like the Great Pyramids at Giza. Furthermore, a French book by Louis Pauwels and Jacques Bergier, *The Morning of the Magicians,* used the lines to advance their theory that astronauts had visited the Earth many thousands of years ago during human prehistory. This alien species had aided human beings in our primeval existence through their highly advanced technology and intelligence, enabling us to break out from the level of other species and take over the planet.

These strange markings are not alone, either. Further south is the largest human figure in the world etched into the side of Solitary Mountain, known as the Giant of Atacama. Elsewhere in South America there are many mountains with depictions of flying birds, spirals and ancient warriorlike beasts. With widely differing interpretations of their meanings, these mysteries are likely to continue for many centuries to come.

# Nazi Gold Stored in Allied Banks

The World Jewish Congress would have it that tons of gold stolen by the Nazis during World War II are still kept in the Federal Reserve Bank of New York and in the Bank of England in London. Furthermore, the organization claims that some of this may have been melted down from the fillings of Holocaust victims' teeth.

This is horrific in itself, but it is in fact only a subplot to a much more disturbing wider conspiracy involving the Swiss banks, which seem to have colluded with the Nazi regime. The Nazis didn't take Switzerland over, and in return, the Swiss took care of their bloodstained stolen treasure.

The World Jewish Congress has taken the situation very seriously ever since it transpired that the authorities in Zurich were hiding accounts of the Holocaust written by Jewish victims. It is now coming out that the Swiss not only colluded with the Nazis during the war but that once the war was over, they only returned 10 percent of the Nazi treasure they were safeguarding.

While it is shocking for a country that claims to be neutral to be condoning Nazi atrocities, what is still more appalling is the discovery that six tons of Nazi gold are currently held by the Bank of England. One document from the U.S. Embassy in Paris stated that one postwar Allied shipment of 8,307 gold bars found in a German salt mine might "represent melted down gold teeth fillings." Although this does not conclusively prove the Nazi gold held by the Allied banks came from the teeth of murdered Jews, it certainly raises the question.

The Swiss government inquiry into the scandal may have been hampered by budget cuts. But on the other hand, investigations may be prevented by a certain reluctance to disclose the truth at all. The Swiss Finance Minister Kaspar Villiger had, in a controversial statement, resolved to cut funds into the investigation from $4.2 million to $2.9 million, a sign that the Swiss were somewhat half-hearted in this matter. But the Federal Reserve chairman Paul Volcker said that a thorough investigation was necessary so that "the issue can be reconciled and put to rest."

A compensation deal has recently been reached, but after fifty years this has come too late for many holocaust survivors and their families.

# The 1973 Oil Embargo

In the aftermath of World War II the United States aided the Japanese in rebuilding their shattered nation. But not entirely surprisingly, the Japanese harbored a certain amount of resentment and entertained thoughts of one day taking over the United States. The most effective way of putting this into action so far as they could see was through the sale of mass-produced goods.

All went according to plan, except on one critical front. The Americans were quite capable of creating mass-produced goods of their own. The car industry could hardly sell to a nation bred on fast cars and cheap gas. So, to achieve their required goals, the Japanese secretly colluded with several Middle Eastern leaders and monarchs, who themselves bore grudges against the United States for aiding and supporting the establishment of Israel.

When all was in place, the Eastern oil barons placed an embargo on the United States. With its supply of gas severely curtailed, Americans turned to Japanese cars, whose chief appeal was excellent fuel consumption. So even if the Japanese didn't actually manage to take over the United States, the plan to make it somewhat dependent on Japan certainly worked as they had hoped.

# Oklahoma City Bombing

The Oklahoma City bombing is completely bewildering, and the authorities have struggled to find some kind of motive behind the violence. Suggestions have included a vengeance for Waco as well as an elaborate anti-Clinton plot, but the action would appear to be rather extreme if this was the case.

A new line of inquiry, however, comes in the form of Mark Koernke. In his video lecture entitled *America in Peril,* he would have his audience believe that the United Nations have launched an invasion of the U.S., claiming that UN troops are pouring into America and hiding in secret military bases. And the headquarters of these secret sites? None other than Oklahoma. Koernke also claims that urban street gangs are being "trained, equipped and uniformed" to be the front line in the American invasion.

According to Koernke, the states of the U.S. will be abolished and the country will be divided into ten regions under the iron fist of the UN. Moreover, as a part of their takeover plan, UN troops intend to lock up Americans in forty-three regional detention camps located throughout the nation. "And," he adds, "the processing center for detainees in the western half of the United States is Oklahoma City."

Newspapers reported that the executed bomber Timothy James McVeigh was one of several bodyguards for Koernke at a Florida appearance last year. If McVeigh and his coconspirators were as close to Koernke as the press would have it, it seems possible that the Oklahoma bombing was meant to be a lethal blow to the supposed UN plot to lock Americans into the aforementioned regional concentration camps.

# Oracle

The Oracle, also called Pythia, at Delphi conjures up mental images of darkness and smoke and above all, a profound wisdom and knowledge. Delphi lies on the slopes of Mount Parnassus in Greece, and the town, once called Kastri, used to lie above the ruins of the sacred compound and was relocated in the 1890s when serious excavation began at the ruins.

Greek myth has it that Zeus sent out two eagles, one to the east and one to the west, to find the center of the Earth. When they then met at Delphi, this indicated where this central point must be. The "omphalos" is a cone-shaped stone and in previous times stood in front of the Temple to mark the "navel" of the Earth.

About 1500 B.C., Mycenaeans settled there and continued the maintenance of the shrine to Gaea, Mother Earth. The Delphic wise women had already gained fame by then. The shrine prospered until five hundred years later when Apollo came down from the north and killed Python, who had been guarding his mother's shrine. Apollo claimed the shrine for himself, and, rid of Gaea's sybils, installed his own oracles.

Centuries before the birth of Christ, faithful travelers were making their way to Delphi to ask for advice from the famous Oracle. Cities considered these trips as an absolute priority and gave generously to help with the funding. For more than six centuries, until the shrine was destroyed by the Christian emperor Arcadius in A.D. 398, Delphi was the center of the spiritual world.

Yet was this a threat to other religions? In the patriarchal climate as it then was, could people cope with the idea of the worship of a goddess? Could a goddess be seen to have the capacity to represent all wisdom? The snake was a powerful symbol of the goddess, and for thousands of years it was greatly respected. Eventually, however, succeeding religions used the snake to represent temptation and therefore something inherently evil. The biblical story of the serpent in the Garden of Eden is an obvious example. Could that story have been written to discourage people from following the advice of the older religion and its leaders? It is a theory that can never be proven one way or the other, but one that is certainly plausible. The Oracle's power and influence being what it was, it certainly would have posed a threat to religions to come.

# The Order of Skull
and Bones

**P**rophecies of a New World Order have been made for
centuries and never quite come to fruition—or at least
not explicitly. From the Illuminati to the Bilderbergs, secret Masonic-style cliques have been rumored to be controlling or seeking to control the direction of world events.

The Order of Skull and Bones is a secret society based
at Yale University in the United States for the males of
prominent families. Its most famous former members allegedly include U.S. President George W. Bush and his father, former president George H. W. Bush. The group's
activities are not known publicly but rumors abound of
clandestine plots to reshape the global order and to influence political figures and institutions. Former members
have gone on to become senators, Supreme Court Justices
and ambassadors, as well as three becoming president. The
famous names who are said to have been through the society include the Rockefellers, Pillsburys, Tafts and, as previously mentioned, the Bushes.

Initially the society was formed to benefit members
when they left college, in a similar manner to the Freemasons. But former Bones members have been accused of

forming a secret government under the guise of intelligence operations, sometimes working against the interests of the president and sometimes carrying out operations in his name. Some of the most famous American scandals have the fingerprints of Bones alumni all over them, from the assassination of JFK to Watergate and the Iran-Contra scandal. The person who some claim to have had a hand in all of these events is George H. W. Bush. During the JFK assassination and the Watergate break-in, Bush was working for the CIA, and during Iran-Contra he was vice president. The influence of former members of this secret society upon American political life takes President Dwight D. Eisenhower's warnings about the corruption of power within the military-industrial complex to whole new levels. It was Eisenhower himself who created this "secret government" under the guise of intelligence operations, a group that conducts its activities in secret for "national security." He appointed Gordon Gray the task of hiding these activities. Gray's son, C. Bowden, was George H. W. Bush's "soul mate" and "protector of the president, come what may." His job was to ensure that Bush was not implicated in the group's activities if any of this became public. Allegations against this secret group include drug trafficking under the veil of the war on drugs, and financing Communism and Hitler's regime.

But one of the most intriguing aspects is that the two major candidates in the 2004 U.S. presidential election, George W. Bush and John Kerry, are both former Bones members. Conspiracies abound that both men are in the pockets of the Bones guiding fathers, so that whoever wins will be able to conduct the clandestine policies of the society for another four years. Furthermore, John Kerry's wife, Teresa, was previously married to John Heinz, another Yale and Skull and Bones alumni member. Heinz was also an outspoken liberal, often voicing views that were not compatible with those of the government. More interestingly, he was part of the commission that looked into the Iran-Contra scandal along with John Tower. Both men saw reams of classified information that implicated the CIA in illegal activity while George H. W. Bush was its director. The two men curiously perished in mysterious plane crashes on successive days in 1991.

Could it be that the Skull and Bones society have exerted their influence over the White House for decades and not only have the ear of the president but are controlling his voice and actions, too? Without any accountability to the American people it could be these behind-the-scenes puppeteers who are really pulling the strings.

# Paul McCartney

In 1969 the rumor that Paul McCartney had died three years earlier raged around the world, coinciding with increasingly widespread suspicion of a conspiracy behind the assassination of JFK. Propagators of the theory claimed that Paul had actually died in a road crash three years earlier, in accordance with the lyrics of the song "A Day in the Life." "He blew his mind out in a car," the lyrics state. "He didn't notice that the lights had changed." And then, even more suspiciously, "A crowd of people stood and stared, they'd seen his face before."

On the cover of the *Sergeant Pepper's Lonely Hearts Club Band* album, the number-plate of one of the cars in the foreground reads "28 IF." If Paul had lived, he would have been 28 by then. Moreover, George Harrison is wearing clothes that clearly resemble an undertaker. In the album itself, at the end of "Strawberry Fields," John Lennon's repeated intonation of the words *cranberry sauce* must surely be a fairly transparent disguise for the words "I bury Paul."

It is said that after Paul's death, the group searched for a replacement so that they could continue with the same success as before. So they drafted in a certain Billy Shears as a replacement, gave him extensive plastic surgery and all grew beards so that no one would actually be able to see the minor facial discrepancies that gave away the fact that he was not the real Paul. If the conspiracy holds, they did a pretty good job of it.

Conspiracy Theories

# Paul Wellstone
# (U.S. Senator)

On October 25, 2002 Paul Wellstone, a progressive U.S. Senator, was killed when his private jet crashed into the ground and burst into flames two miles short of its destination in Minnesota. Reports initially suggested that mechanical failure was to blame for the disaster, but some believe that Wellstone was the victim of a political assassination. Never shy to voice his opinions, the liberal Democrat was a well-publicized opponent of George Bush's war resolution, the only senator, in fact, to vote against it.

Investigators concluded that none of the typical causes of a small plane accident—engine failure, icing, pilot error—caused the plane to crash. And while weather conditions were less than ideal, with some ice and freezing rain, visibility was well above the minimum required, between two and two and a half miles. Although the approach to the airport was being made using instruments, the airport would have been in clear view of the pilot once he descended below the lowest cloud layer at about seven hundred feet.

Under different political circumstances one would dismiss Wellstone's death as a tragic accident whose cause, even if it cannot be precisely determined, lies in the sphere of aircraft engineering and weather phenomena. But, interestingly, Wellstone's death came almost two years to the day after a similar plane crash killed another Democratic Senate hopeful, Missouri governor Mel Carnahan, on October 16, 2000.

# Pearl Harbor

One of the defining moments of World War II was the Japanese "surprise" attack on Pearl Harbor, which brought the United States into the war. Without this attack and without American involvement in Western Europe, the shape of the postwar world may well have been entirely different.

But was the attack on Pearl Harbor in December 1941 really a surprise? There is plenty of documented evidence suggesting that President Franklin D. Roosevelt knew about the planned attack and kept it secret to promote his war-time ambitions. Roosevelt was keen to involve America in the war in Western Europe but was restrained by public opinion, which ran at 88 percent against joining the Allies. In addition, he had promised during his reelection campaign: "I have said this before, but I shall say it again and again and again: Your boys are not going to be sent into any foreign wars." But in private he planned for American troops to go to war to help fight for freedom.

In the months and years leading up to the attack America had continuously provoked Japan by freezing her assets, halting exports, employing an embargo and refusing access to the Panama Canal for Japanese ships. In his war diary of October 16, 1941, Secretary of War Henry Stimson wrote: "We face the delicate question of the diplomatic fencing to be done so as to be sure Japan is put into the wrong and makes the first bad move—overt move." A month later he wrote, "The question was how we should maneuver them [the Japanese] into the position of firing the first shot."

In order to prepare for the attack, or more accurately to *not* prepare for it, the commanders at Pearl Harbor were not made aware of the vital intelligence being gleaned in Washington. Of most importance was Washington's ability to crack Japan's secret diplomatic code, known as "Purple." This highly encrypted code was cracked by American signals intelligence in 1940 and was swiftly used to read Japanese diplomatic communications. Copies of this intelligence were not passed to commanders at Pearl Harbor, however, despite its obvious vulnerability to attack and complaints from the armed forces based there. An interception made on November 11 warned, "The situation is nearing a climax, and the time is getting short."

Equally, when the Japanese naval fleet approached Hawaii, it has always been claimed that it had complete radio silence, making it undetectable. But the following interception was made from a dispatch from Admiral Yamamoto to the Japanese First Air Fleet on November 26, 1941: "The task force, keeping its movement strictly secret and maintaining close guard against submarines and aircraft, shall advance into Hawaiian waters, and upon the very opening of hostilities shall attack the main force of the United States fleet and deal it a mortal blow. The first air raid is planned for the dawn of x-day. Exact date to be given by later order." These clear warnings were never acted upon by the U.S. Navy, in a chain of command that led ultimately to the president. Despite repeated warnings from Dutch, Korean and British agents about a possible attack, the U.S. government showed either incredible ineptitude or deliberately overlooked the threat.

Furthermore, all merchant shipping in the Western Pacific was halted on the day of the attack, presumably to avoid the Japanese fleet being spotted and the alarm being raised, which would thus ruin FDR's careful plan. Because once the Pearl Harbor attack took place, the American public would demand swift and immediate retribution.

The Commission that looked into the attacks was composed of cronies loyal to Roosevelt, who decided that the attacks were a "dereliction of duty" by the Hawaiian commanders—the same commanders to whom Washington had denied intelligence briefings. With public anger directed toward them and toward Japan, the real culprits were allowed to proceed with their previously unpopular war plan.

# Piet Mondrian

The De Stijl movement in painting originated in the Netherlands, with Piet Mondrian and Theo van Doesburg as two of its main instigators. At first glance, De Stijl may have appeared to be an artistic movement centered around the creation of art generated for all people regardless of background and the acceptance of art by the masses, many of whom remained skeptical of modern styles. But behind this seemingly benign and philanthropic concept of art, the painters were actually putting across hidden messages meant to influence the minds of their viewers. Of these painters, Mondrian proved the most subversive and potentially dangerous.

Mondrian carefully arranged lines and blocks of colors to produce a style that he felt communicated the most fundamental and universal elements of the visual world. In doing so, he created small patterns, barely perceptible to the naked eye, which would play with the audience's sense of vision. At the intersection of the black lines, gray dots would appear to the viewer. The lines, juxtaposed against a white background and blocks of primary color, gave the paintings a three-dimensional illusion and appeared to move forwards and backwards in space. In addition, several viewers noticed that the lines would stop just short of the edge of the canvas. It was in these areas of his works that Mondrian placed his hidden messages, directing the viewer towards a sense of peace and harmony.

Over time, Mondrian programmed the viewer to accept messages of a new world order, which would promote a peaceful, classless society based on images of harmony and inner contentment. As he grew older, Mondrian increased the complexity of his works while holding on to the same fundamental artistic practices. However, some theorists express concerns that Mondrian used his paintings to exert a darker influence over the masses his work is aimed at. If this is true, Mondrian may well have harbored aspirations to brainwash an entire society.

# Pisa's Leaning Tower

During the Middle Ages and the Renaissance, it was the Italian cities that dominated the cultural landscape of the Mediterranean. The Italians spared no expense in maintaining their cultural prowess and spent enormous amounts of money decorating their churches and cathedrals, which were often the central points of Italian cities. Pisa was no exception. The city's power reached its peak directly after the turn of the first millennium, and the citizens put all their energies into erecting an intricate display of church buildings, starting with the cathedral and continuing with the baptistry. The buildings used the finest materials and craftsmen available and were widely acclaimed for their beauty. But such success, both on the cultural and financial levels, obviously bred a certain amount of resentment among Pisa's enemies, particularly among the Venetians who liked to see themselves as the leading forces of Southern Europe.

Their jealousy grew and grew so that they started to fabricate elaborate plots against the city. During the construction of the Campanile (or bell tower) at Pisa, Venetian vandals weakened the foundation so that after the completion of a few stories the tower began to tip. The Pisan architects attempted to make up for this by curving the upper floors, but with no success. Their pride was sorely wounded, and their confidence knocked. They declined as a naval power, while the Venetians, having achieved what they set out to do, prospered and grew to become the dominant power in the western Mediterranean.

# Pope John Paul I

To appreciate the possible causes behind the murder of
Pope John Paul I it is necessary to put it in the context
of the nineteenth century when the Catholic Church was
stripped of its powers by the Italian national revolution.
Pope Pius IX, then in power, compensated for his loss of
earthly land and power by ordering the Vatican Council to
pass the doctrine of unquestionable papal infallibility.

Pope Pius XI received the equivalent of £40 million and
a restoration of what was, effectively, a spell of power in
the Vatican City. Both he and his successors were to exploit
and manipulate this arrangement entirely to their own advantage. One means of doing this was in the creation of a
Vatican Bank, which was quite beyond the reach of any legal organization, secular or sacred. It was thus ideal for
evading tax and engaging in underhand financial activities.

Under the doctrine established by the Vatican Council I,
the Pope's word, however corrupt, was law and any deviation
was false. Once the Vatican Council II was in place, it faced
severe opposition from conservatives within the Catholic
ranks. As long as the Pope's word was law, there was no
threat to the established order of things. Once free thought

was encouraged, the whole infrastructure of the Vatican was under threat. And once the structure of the Vatican was under threat, it was not simply an issue of discussing reforms to the liturgy and the pros and cons of artificial birth control, but far more importantly, the financial advantages enjoyed by the members of the Vatican.

The conservatives and reformers reached more and more of an impasse after the death of John XXIII in 1963, and this resulted in the election of Paul VI who agonized over the morality of artificial birth control. The liberalism of Vatican Council II was certainly not welcomed with open arms on a universal level. Old ways were safe and many looked back at the more rigid doctrine of the pre–John XXIII era with nostalgia.

Pope John Paul I's modest and self-effacing demeanor appealed to the conservatives who saw him as a perfect compromise candidate, whom they could effectively control. And yet, once elected, the new Pope began to display a charisma that had been hidden by his former reserve. He devoted himself entirely to revolutionizing the papacy and to returning it to its spiritual origins. He refused to be sucked into the empty ritual of his predecessors and refused to follow the scripts prepared for him by the conservatives at his press conferences. The conservative factions began to despair, especially after he began to express positive views on contraception. The final straw came when the newly elected Pope started to delve into the Vatican Bank's dealings.

Uncovering a whole network of corruption involving the Mafia, bribery and extortion, John Paul called Cardinal Villott, the leader of the powerful conservative Curia, to his study to discuss certain changes that he intended to put into action. Several people were going to be forced to "resign." Among these were the head of the Vatican Bank and several members of the Curia, including Villott himself. Moreover, Villott was told, the Pope would also call a meeting with an American delegation to discuss a reconsideration of the Church's position on birth control.

By the time the Pope retired for the night on the evening of September 28, 1978, taking with him the paperwork that would reveal the Vatican's dealings with the Mafia, he had made himself more enemies than ever. And when his house-keeper tried to rouse him early the next morning, there was no reply. Returning a while later, she found the Pope sitting in bed with an awful grimace on his face, the papers still in his hand. Beside him lay a bottle of pills for his blood pressure, and vomit covered the sheets. Her first port of call was Villott. Villott did not even check the news but summoned the doctor immediately. Having done so, he made haste to the Pope's rooms and gathered the bottle of pills along with the precious papers. That was the last that was seen of either item.

There is still no public death certificate for the Pope. Although Italian law requires a period of at least twenty-four hours before a body may be embalmed, Villott made sure that the Pope's body was embalmed within twelve hours. And while the convention for embalming a body dictates that the blood and internal organs be removed, the Pope's corpse was left as it was. Hence no one was able to verify whether the body had been poisoned or not.

# Pope John Paul II

On May 13, 1981 antipapal violence became even more overt as Pope John Paul II was shot and very nearly killed in St. Peter's Square. Immediately it was accepted by people all over the world as the action of an individual madman called Mehmet Ali Agca. Even at the time, Italian authorities suggested that this might be a part of a larger conspiracy, but this was largely ignored. The Western press suggested that Mehmet Ali Agca may in fact have been a cog in the wheel of a Turkish right-wing Islamic fundamentalist conspiracy, but this was as far as it went. New evidence, however, has pointed the finger at the Soviet KGB, operating through the secret factions of the Communist regimes in Bulgaria and the Turkish Mafia. Rumor has it that Agca escaped from a Turkish prison and, having been given extensive training and an elaborate plot, adopted a right-wing disguise to hide the real motivations of the assassination.

The plot to kill the Pope may have failed, but this may not have been the sole purpose of the assassination attempt. The whole thing could have been a clever double bluff. After all, what better way to stir up public reaction against right-wing extremity and religious "fundamentalism." No one suspected the Communist role for a minute.

This does raise some doubts as to whether the neo-Nazi activities that have plagued Germany for more than half a century are in fact propagated by extreme right-wing factions at all or whether, again, it could be Communists behind the series of events, which have included the branding of the swastika, militant homophobia and racial prejudice. Information leaked from within the Soviet Party revealed that one of its primary aims was to stir up public emotion against all that it termed as right-wing. Hitlerites were one obvious example, but other right-wing factions also included Christians, liberals and in fact anyone at all who was not Communist.

# Population Control

One would hope that Hitler's "ethnic cleansing" would be a thing of the past. But not so. Dr. Len Horowitz's book *Emerging Viruses* reveals a terrifying program in American bio-warfare labs in collusion with the medical industry.

Horowitz has uncovered the hard evidence that proves that hepatitis B vaccines infected with the live AIDS virus had been targeted at homosexuals and blacks in New York, San Francisco and Central Africa (via the UN's World Health Organization). This is precisely where the AIDS virus exploded from.

On a much less specific level, Horowitz details how the entire baby boom generation was injected with polio vaccines, which may have protected them against polio, but has increased their chances of succumbing to cancer several fold. The vaccines being laced with live cancer viruses, it is estimated that one in three of the population unfortunate enough to be born around the baby boom period will develop cancer.

The hundreds of ways designed to kill the members of the population termed as "useless eaters" would be quite ingenious if it were not so horrific. The wide range of vaccines that are accepted completely unquestioned are a prime culprit. Horowitz relays how the designer experimental viruses in the vaccines given to the soldiers prior to the Gulf War are directly responsible for the syndrome that has already hit more than 200,000 veterans and is fast spreading among their wives and children.

Another direct form of population control, which few people even consider, comes in the form of heavily processed chemical food, bringing millions to the fast food industries every year. Advertising does its job and people seem too set in their ways to realize the damage that this does, intentionally or not.

Of course, it would be a little extreme to suggest that all disease is manufactured by an army of Men in Black, although there are some who would not dispute this. But the fact remains that more than one million people die prematurely every year because the health care system cares far more for the creation and treatment of disease than it does for its prevention in the first place.

# Port Chicago Disaster

In 1944 the Port Chicago disaster in America killed hundreds of Americans in a matter of seconds. On the night of July 17 two ships loading ammunition in the port's naval base were destroyed in a gigantic explosion. The loading pier and the two ships were immediately destroyed and the nearby town of Port Chicago was also badly damaged. More than three hundred American sailors were killed outright. Several hundred more were badly injured and the cost of the property damage was enormous. It was easily the worst Allied disaster of World War II. Officially the world's first nuclear test took place at Alamogordo in New Mexico, but speculation has arisen as to whether the Port Chicago blast may in fact have been an atomic experiment.

It was at this time that specifications for the U-235 bomb used at Hiroshima were completed. Hardware for at least three bombs had been ordered by the end of March 1944, and by the previous December, 74 kilograms of uranium were available. The American government claimed that the explosion could not have been caused by a bomb as there was not enough uranium available for construction, but based on the above evidence, this would seem to be a lie. In fact, 15.5 kilograms of uranium is all that is needed to build an atomic bomb. If a nuclear weapon was tested at Port Chicago, it is likely to have been one of those built after March 1944.

The total disintegration of the ships and the widespread destruction would suggest that the force of the blast was far greater than even hundreds of tons of high explosives could have caused. Witnesses told of a blinding white flash reaching millions of degrees centigrade in millionths of a second, which is now known to be characteristic of nuclear explosions. Moreover, the typical nuclear fireball and condensation cloud also point to atomic testing.

# Queen Elizabeth I

No one has ever known quite why Elizabeth I should not have married. Certainly an air of ambiguity seems to lie over that part of her life: not only would this state of affairs have been perceived as undesirable, but it was quite unthinkable not to provide an immediate heir to the throne. For years, speculations have been afloat that the queen was in fact malformed and that her inability to produce children was only one manifestation of her dysfunctional sexuality.

This has been taken one step further by some historians who claim that Elizabeth was in fact a man. There is no doubting that this was disguise at its most artful if this was the case, but it would provide one answer as to why she never married. The theory runs that at the tender age of two or three, the infant queen went to stay with some distant cousins. Falling ill while she was there, she could not be saved and she died. Terrified of incurring the wrath of her father, Henry, who would have beheaded them without hesitation, the family dressed up a little boy to take her place. This charade continued, apparently, until her death and would explain why she was bald, as well as her celibacy.

This raises somewhat disturbing questions about which other celebrities are actually transsexual. Maybe discretion is the better part of valor.

# Rennes-Le-Château

The appearance of the book *The Holy Blood and the Holy Grail*, written by Michael Baigent, Henry Lincoln and Richard Leigh in 1982, sparked off waves of controversy throughout the Western world. Lincoln's discovery of the unsolved mysteries shrouding the tiny French hamlet of Rennes-le-Château has unveiled possible webs of conspiracy spiraling back to the birth of Christ. Could new light be thrown on the last two thousand years of our history?

The first mystery surrounds the parish priest in the village at the end of the nineteenth century. His name was Berenger Saunière. Between 1885 and 1891 his salary averaged very much what one would expect from a rural curate at the time, and he led a quiet, ordinary life. For a long time he had wanted to restore the village church, which stood on the foundations of a much older structure dating back from the sixth century. It was in a state of almost hopeless disrepair. Funded modestly by the village, Saunière embarked upon a plan of restoration, finding inside one of the hollow altar columns four parchments preserved in sealed wooden tubes. The parchments consisted of a series of seemingly incomprehensible codes, but with time their messages became clearer. The raised letters in the second parchment spelled out a coherent message: TO DAGOBERT II AND TO SION BELONGS THIS TREASURE AND HE IS THERE DEAD. Although unsure about its meaning, Saunière realized that he had stumbled across something of importance and immediately went to Paris. Saunière spent three weeks there. What happened is unknown, but we do know that he, a provincial country priest, was welcomed into the most distinguished ecclesiastical circles.

It was after this trip that the mystery started to thicken. Lincoln shows that, for a start, Saunière's expenditure seemed to go far beyond his means. By the end of his life in 1917, it is calculated that he had spent millions of francs, often in seemingly bizarre ways. The church was redecorated, but redecorated in the most unconventional way, so that above the doorway, a Latin inscription bore the message: TERRIBILIS EST LOCUS ISTE (THIS PLACE IS TERRIBLE) and the garish frescoes on the church walls all seemed to deviate from biblical teaching. In the Ninth Station of the Cross, for example, which shows Jesus' body being carried into the tomb, there is a background of a full moon. What message was being put across here? The Bible would have it that Jesus' burial occurred during the afternoon, so is this simply an interpretation that the burial actually happened at nightfall? Or is it a representation of the body being carried into the tomb at all? Could it be in fact the depiction of Jesus being carried out of rather than into the tomb?

Saunière's life became more and more mysterious. His entry into the upper ranks of Parisian society seemed incongruous to say the least, but this did not pose as many questions as the Church's intense interest in his findings, or his subsequent exemption from the Vatican. Rumor has it that on being called to give last rites to Saunière, the neighboring parish priest fled from Saunière's sickroom, visibly distraught, and refused to perform the ceremony. According to one witness he never smiled again. And why should his housekeeper, Marie Denarnaud, who became his life-time companion, have referred to a "secret" that would give her not only wealth but also power?

It could have been that Saunière had stumbled across a huge sum of money somewhere in the proceedings. But Henry Lincoln explores the possibility that he had come across something far more explosive, indeed dangerous. Could it be that he had come across knowledge that would affect the entire Western vision and history? Could his money have been part of a vast ecclesiastical blackmail? Or even a payment for silence? Whatever the answer, the Vatican appeared to be afraid of him throughout his life-time, and waited on his every command. Whether he was blackmailing them we do not know, but he did appear to have an influence that extended far beyond the provincial backwater of Rennes-le-Château. On his deathbed he passed the secret to his housekeeper. She took the secret to her grave. The mystery continues.

# Rennes-Le-Château 2: The Church

Henry Lincoln says himself that he never set out to discredit the tenets of Christianity, but his research, inspired by the mystery surrounding Saunière, points to a network of conspiracy and obscurity that cannot help but throw the entire Christian culture into question. His hypothesis revolves around the fact that Jesus was in fact married. There is no explicit statement in the Gospels to support this, but if he was claiming the status of Rabbi, this would almost be a prerequisite. Jewish law stated quite categorically that an unmarried man may not be a teacher. Moreover, the account of the Wedding of Cana raises questions as to whether this ceremony was in fact Jesus' own wedding. The presence of Mary, the mother of Jesus, for a start. And the repeated references to the bridegroom addressed to Jesus. One could conclude that Jesus and the bridegroom are the same person.

Lincoln goes on to show how if he was married, biblical evidence would seem either to point to Mary Magdalene, whose role throughout the Gospels seems deliberately ambiguous, or to Mary of Bethany as being his wife. There is also the suggestion that the two Marys were actually the same person. As Lincoln points out, the medieval Church and popular tradition definitely regarded them as such. One woman, recurring throughout the Gospels under different names and performing different roles, could have been the wife of Jesus.

And if Jesus was married, could this have been a marriage to establish a dynasty, a dynasty that would have threatened the entire Roman order?

The question of whether Jesus did father children is, again, far from explicit in the Gospels, but, following Lincoln's argument, one can question the status of Barrabus. If Jesus had had a son, it is indeed likely that he would be called "Jesus bar Rabbi," "Jesus, son of the Rabbi." Alternatively, "Jesus bar Abba," "Jesus the son of the father" might again refer to Jesus' son, if he were indeed the Heavenly Father.

And the whole issue of the Crucifixion is again fraught with ambiguity, as Lincoln shows. Crucifixion was a Roman practice and was reserved exclusively for those who had committed crimes against the empire. This would suggest that he must have done something to provoke the wrath of the Roman empire, rather than the Jewish law. Moreover, victims of crucifixion usually took over a week to die, and yet Jesus' death seems to have been well-timed to fit in with Old Testament prophecy. And according to Roman law, a crucified man was denied burial and simply left on the cross to rot.

If Jesus did not die on the cross, what happened to him and where did he go? Did the resurrection ever actually take place, or was this all part of the grand escape on the part of Jesus? According to certain Eastern legends, he lived until he was well into his seventies, and, Lincoln argues, the documents found by Saunière at Rennes-le-Château contained "incontrovertible proof that Jesus was still alive in A.D. 45. And quite apart from what happened to him, what happened to his family? If he was indeed married with children, escape would have been as imperative for them as it was for him. Lincoln goes on to ask whether

they could have escaped into the South of France. Could
Jesus' mummified body even be somewhere near Rennes-
le-Château? And could they have brought the dynasty of
Jesus into France? Was Jesus' familial descendency in fact
no more miraculous than any of the rest of us? Obviously,
one cannot point at any one individual as a direct descen-
dent of Jesus, but if this is the case, it would seem that the
entire values and thinking of the Western world would be
severely challenged.

Saunière's secret was well-kept. But did he unearth a
huge cover-up on the part of the Church, obscured by legend, and lost in time? One can see why the Church at the end
of the nineteenth century was so anxious that he should not
speak out.

# Robert Maxwell

The web of intrigue that surrounded Robert Maxwell throughout his life only began to unravel after his death in November 1991. While soaking up the sun aboard his yacht in the Canary Islands, he mysteriously vanished overboard, just as revelations about his dubious financial dealings began to emerge. The former Mirror Group chairman and pension thief was allegedly involved in a $40 billion money-laundering operation with the Russian Mafia and a group of Chinese Triads. He was also close to conspirators in the coup against Russian President Mikhail Gorbachev in 1991, and was on the periphery of the Iran-Contra affair. At the same time, he moved with ease among the world's powerbrokers and had access to the most secretive places in the world, including the Oval Office and the Kremlin. Given his controversial and dangerous background, it is hardly surprising that his death, to this day, is shrouded in mystery.

Numerous conspiracy theories exist about Maxwell's "assassination," many of which tend to mix the fanciful with the factual. The most popular school of thought claims that he died due to his close association with Mossad, the

Israeli Secret Service. It is alleged that Mossad agents chose to eliminate Maxwell because he was threatening to expose Israeli state secrets. Indeed, the death has all the hallmarks of a Mossad operation. According to supporters of the Mossad theory, Israeli agents boarded Maxwell's yacht, the *Lady Ghislaine,* under the cover of darkness and plunged a needle filled with a lethal nerve serum into his neck. They then lowered his body into the sea to make his death seem like a suicide.

As well as working for Israel, Maxwell was a conduit for the Communist Secret Services, setting up countless companies on behalf of former members of the KGB, East German Stasi and Bulgarian government. It is also suspected that Eastern European crime bosses and governments swallowed up billions of Maxwell's laundered money after his death. Such information only fuels speculation that Maxwell's death was not a suicide but the clinical work of assassins.

# Roswell

What really happened at Roswell? No other UFO incident has attracted as much attention as the event here in 1947. The proponents' case is that at least one, possibly two, flying saucers crashed in New Mexico during July of that year and that a rancher named Mac Brazel found some of the debris from the crash. The alien wreckage and the bodies of its inhabitants were retrieved immediately and taken away for further investigation. No one knows what happened to them, but no one seemed very keen to divulge any information, suggesting that whatever had been discovered was quite possibly of enormous danger to our civilization.

The whole case lay forgotten until 1978 when Stanton Friedman and William L. Moore rediscovered the Roswell reports and pieced together irrefutable evidence that Brazel had indeed found parts of an alien spacecraft. They worked out a flight path for the UFO: that it came from somewhere southeast of Roswell, suffered some kind of damage or accident over Brazel's ranch where it shed some debris, then veered west to crash in the desert in the region of St. Agustin. It was made very clear to them, however, that the

U.S. authorities would be no more forthcoming than
they had been thirty years earlier. And it was not just the
government who seemed determined to keep something
undercover. When Lydia Sleppy, a teletype operator in Albuquerque, was putting reports of the crashed saucer onto
the air, her machine ground to a halt. Then, says *The
Roswell Incident* (Friedmann and Moore, 1980), it came
out with this curt message: ATTENTION ALBUQUERQUE: DO
NOT TRANSMIT. REPEAT DO NOT TRANSMIT THIS MESSAGE.
STOP COMMUNICATION IMMEDIATELY. The sender was not
identified.

Someone does not want the truth of the incident to be
revealed. And so, we can ask, was the crashed object really
an alien craft? Or could there be a very dark and dreadful
secret behind what really went on?

Of course, the object could have been a balloon, either a
weather balloon or the test launch of a balloon in the top secret Project Mogul. According to surviving project members
of Mogul, a large number of these balloons could certainly
have crashed onto Brazel's ranch, and their remains would
fit his description of what he found. Mogul's classified purpose was to try and develop a way to monitor possible Soviet
nuclear waves, and no other means of investigating the nuclear activities of a closed country like the USSR was yet
available. The project was given a high priority. And yet the
whole Roswell mystery could be no more than a military
failure to tell a balloon from an alien flying saucer.

However, there are more unnerving possibilities. Suppose the balloon was the top-secret device that was going
to win the Cold War for the U.S. Suppose it crashed on
its first flight, and suppose a serious investigation would
reveal that it was hopeless with no future and only went
ahead because of a network of corrupt government contracts and dealings. Or suppose that there is a still more
murky Roswell secret, such as a tethered balloon carrying
a nuclear device designed to explode at high altitude. Suppose it broke free, depositing its lethal cargo near Roswell,
the town avoiding complete destruction by only a tiny

margin. This would be the kind of event that people would go to any length to hide, even by creating elaborate UFO contact stories once the investigations started.

In 1948, the year after the Roswell incident, Newman, a British writer, produced a book whose theme was uncomfortably close to the events of the year before. It told of a faked UFO crash by leading world scientists whose aim it was to force world disarmament. Some believe Newman alluded to the events of the previous year, and if so, this would suggest that what happened at Roswell may have carried a political agenda—or even that the incident was spelling out some kind of warning.

# Rudolf Hess

One of the enduring mysteries of World War II was precisely the role played by Rudolf Hess and what his ultimate fate was. A book published in the United States in 2002 claims that "for sixty years an unprecedented conspiracy has existed at the highest levels of the British Establishment to prevent the truth about Rudolf Hess and his fateful flight to Scotland in May 1941 from surfacing into the public domain."

Hess was the Deputy Führer and first in line to succeed Adolf Hitler. In 1941 he flew to Britain, unarmed, and landed in Scotland, where he was promptly arrested. He has popularly been portrayed as a lunatic on a one-man mission. The book alleges that he actually arrived in Scotland with the full knowledge and support of Hitler, acting as his personal envoy. It is argued that he was to meet a member of the royal family to organize a peace treaty between Britain and Germany. Hitler was thought to want to avoid conflict with Britain if he could because he understood how difficult it would be to conquer the island, with simultaneous Eastern and Western fronts an enormous drain on his military machine, settling for continental Europe as the limit of his imperialist ambitions.

When Winston Churchill got wind of this plan, however, he was determined to prevent its success. Churchill had been an impassioned critic of Hitler, and his disgust of the German appeasers within Britain had instilled a belligerent streak within him towards Nazi Germany, which he viewed as a scourge on the face of Europe he was determined to defeat. He instructed the army to imprison Hess as soon as he arrived on British soil.

In a further twist, it is claimed that Hess used an anonymous double. Whilst the fake Hess was kept in a Welsh prison, the real one was still in Scotland. This prevented any rescue attempts on him by German special forces. In an attempt to undermine Churchill, the Duke of Kent—part of the establishment keen on a peace deal with Hitler—flew to Iceland for a break. On his journey he stopped off in Scotland to collect the real Hess and take him to Sweden to initiate a peace plan. Intriguingly, the plane crashed on leaving Scotland and those on board were killed instantly.

The motive for those in the aristocracy was simple. They viewed the Nazi threat as being much less important than the threat from the Soviet Union. They thought that if they could enable Hitler to concentrate all his efforts on the Eastern Front he would have greater success in defeating Stalin's empire. This would leave both the Soviets and the Germans severely weakened, with a power and territorial vacuum in Western Europe ready to be exploited by the British.

With the Duke of Kent's plan foiled, it was simply left for the fake Hess to take the stand at the Nuremberg trials, where Hermann Goering claimed: "Hess? Which Hess? The Hess you have here? Our Hess? Your Hess?" Despite this, the government and establishment of the time managed to conceal this elaborate plan and counter-plan amidst the euphoria of the Allies' war victory, when people preferred to look forward towards a more optimistic future.

# Santa

The claim that Santa is the devil is a little frightening as he infiltrates our Western culture and our children's minds every Christmastime. Santa gets away with it because his methods are subtle. He still frightens kids; it's just that he does so on their own terms. The warning that, if they aren't good, Santa won't bring them any presents isn't so far off from religious threats that unless you do X, Y or Z you will go to hell.

And there's more. Santa comes down the chimney. And the devil apparently lives in a pit of hell-fire. No one has ever been to and returned alive from either hell or Santa's workshop. And they are both worshipped. The fact that Santa commands adoration from small children and the devil from certain heavy-metal freaks is beside the point, especially when one considers that Santa's reindeer have cloven feet.

And most disturbingly of all, Santa's name can be no mistake. It is a not very well-disguised anagram of Satan, which is surely not mere coincidence. Who can tell which Christmas time Santa will choose to reveal his true identity?

# School Lunch

Stodge and grease galore, the school lunch is not the most enticing of prospects. And what is more, its innocent victims who have to endure it every day are blissfully unaware that they are acting as the pawns in a massive government conspiracy over which they have absolutely no control.

Stodge and grease aside, the boiled cabbage and meat loaf are priced extortionately. This is all part of the plan. Shoveling platefuls of the stuff down their victims' throats, the government makes millions of dollars from the companies that produce these delectable offerings. At the time, the gruesome effects of the conspiracy are not to be seen. But in five years the kids will come to regret all those jelly donuts eaten in their youth and will start to develop a fat complex. So, the cycle starts all over again. The government collaborates with drug companies and sells drugs to make you lose weight for an exorbitant amount of money. And what happens then? The victims become addicted to the drugs and the government makes more and more money until they die.

By now the conspirators have made enough to run away and live it up elsewhere. Of course, without them, the country will wither away and they can then come back as right-wing dictators.

# Shergar's Mysterious Disappearance

The kidnapping of champion racehorse Shergar remains one of Britain's most baffling whodunnits. For two decades, the disappearance of the celebrated Derby winner has been shrouded in a fog of mystery and conspiracy theories. On February 8, 1983, armed men burst into Shergar's stable in Ballymany, County Kildare, and forced head groom Jim Fitzgerald to load the horse onto a vehicle, which was then towed away. Shergar was never seen again. Days later, Fitzgerald received an anonymous ransom demand of £2 million for the safe return of the champion wonder horse. But Shergar's primary owner, the Aga Khan, refused to give in for fear of setting a precedent in the sport. Shergar's vet, Stan Cosgrove, believes the kidnappers made the mistake of thinking that the Aga Khan was the sole owner of the horse and would be only too willing to part with his millions. In fact, Shergar was owned by thirty-four separate individuals in a syndicate, most of whom had no intention of paying up.

A former gunman with the Irish Republican Army (IRA) recently confessed that the IRA was behind the bungled kidnapping, but the group has never accepted responsibility for the crime. Even so, Shergar was taken at the height of the IRA's military campaign against the British, and at a time when it was desperate for funds to buy weapons. Given its plight at the time, a theft of such magnitude seems far from implausible.

Over the last twenty years there have been numerous reported sightings of Shergar, but none have proved conclusive. Some claim to have seen him racing in Libya, others believe that gunrunners took him to Marseille. Conspiracy theories abound, too, concerning Mafia involvement.

Shergar's kidnapping remains one of the greatest mysteries of the 1980s. To this day, no body has been found. The case remains open.

# Smuggling

In various cities in Canada, city councils have introduced new laws to criminalize tobacco smoking. This coincides with a nationwide attempt to reduce tobacco advertising and sponsorship. In Vancouver, all restaurants have a smoke-free policy and many municipalities have forbidden smoking in bars and pubs.

But it seems quite clear that the instigators of this regime could profit considerably from it. During the alcohol prohibition in America, it became rapidly obvious that if alcohol was smuggled over the border from Canada, it could then be sold at grossly inflated prices to an ever-present market, thereby making far more money than if it were legal. Apparently certain highly placed individuals bribed government officials to keep the prohibition in place.

Who could profit from the illegalization of tobacco? Tobacco in Canada is sold for a hugely inflated price. Cigarettes are hijacked from incoming vehicles, stolen from grocery stores and smuggled from eastern to western Canada.

People wouldn't smuggle unless it made them money.

And so, we can ask, are organized criminal groups bribing the Canadian government to illegalize tobacco products so that they can make more money by selling smuggled goods?

# Smurfs

**M**yth has it that *The Smurfs* is just a harmless children's cartoon program. But could it actually be a plot by the National Broadcasting Company to increase television viewing by promoting anti-intellectual propaganda? Or could the program be even more corrupt in encouraging an authoritarian state where individual thought is discouraged?

The Smurfs' way of life may appear to be idyllic, and there is certainly none of the unpleasantness that may plague other societies and civilizations. However, this peaceable attitude is not democratic but dictatorial, and while Papa Smurf may come across as a benign, rather bumbling old fool, his subjects must be wary of their future should their leader's kindly nature change. And the question of quite how he wields his power must also be addressed—Smurf incest, it would appear, is rampant, and one does start to wonder whether in fact Papa Smurf fathered the whole village. Moreover, he seems to be completely lacking in any kind of forethought, because in denying anyone any access to the library, and thus any development in individual thought, there will be a bit of a problem once he dies. And he can't pretend to himself that he will carry on forever. There will be no one to replace him. Perhaps the Smurf dynasty will only have a limited run.

Smurf illiteracy is widespread, even if this is not stated explicitly. It's certainly not the popular thing to admit to being able to read even if you can actually do so, with the sole exception of Brainy Smurf, whose erudite tidbits of information ostracize him completely from the village. His readings are clearly not appreciated by the community, and even Papa Smurf only keeps up a clever appearance of studying his books of magic. His magic spells are all actually a complete sham, as he had to look them all up, and while he claims to be studying, he is in fact otherwise engaged, sometimes, it would seem, in the company of Smurfette.

The hand of the village's only female, not to say demi-goddess, provokes ongoing rivalry. Hefty Smurf is himself a demi-god, and Handy Smurf, if not blessed with good looks, is the epitome of manual dexterity, and it would seem that they stand the most chance. Poor old Poet and Brainy Smurf don't seem to be the village Casanovas.

Moreover, vocabulary is reduced to an all-time low, freedom of expression is stamped upon and all communication is molded into the official party line. The Smurf language seems to operate on the grammatical basis that the word *"smurf "* does for any other word and can be substituted for any part of speech if the correct word is elusive. Even the Smurf National Anthem is somewhat restricted, consisting only of one word, going along the lines of "La la la la la la la la la la la la la la la la . . ." The complete lack of intellectual and technological progress in the immobile Smurf society seems to be a fairly transparently veiled message to viewers that they should become passive and completely devoid of initiative.

By indoctrinating its youngest viewers with a scorn for education, the program was effectively planning a nation of couch potatoes who would not question the way of things. One student commented, "I always knew there was something funny about that show. My parents never wanted me to watch it. They actually preferred that I watch other programs full of senseless violence. Now I know why."

# Space Shuttle *Columbia*

Whenever a tragic event occurs, it is customary for a conspiracy theory to follow swiftly after. This similarly applied to the events of February 1, 2003 when the NASA space shuttle *Columbia* exploded upon reentry to the Earth's orbit following a successful space mission. But whether the incident was a mere accident or the result of something far more disquieting, there were plenty of coincidences involved for cynics to create a circumstantial case for the latter.

Despite the crash taking place in Texas, the main focus of curiosity centred on a potential link to the Arab-Israeli conflict in the Middle East. The vapor trails from the disintegrating aircraft were first seen over the town of Palestine, Texas, which is also where the first debris was found. One of the six crewmembers on board was Colonel Ilan Ramon, Israel's first-ever astronaut. Ramon was a former Israeli Air Force pilot, who participated in the bombing of Iraq's Osirak nuclear reactor in 1981. The crash took place against the backdrop of the military build-up of U.S. and coalition forces in anticipation of the Iraq War and increasing hostility in the Middle East to the United States and the enemies of the Arab world, primarily Israel. With fierce Arab condemnation of Israel's occupation of the West Bank and as they see it the persecution of the Palestinian people, the irony of the crash location, Palestine, Texas, seems too much of a coincidence for some.

For those who like to create or uncover anti-Zionist conspiracies, these facts seem to point to only one thing: divine intervention. Palestinian terrorist organizations described it as "punishment from Allah." Many of those who believe in a connection are active Holocaust-deniers, and they seized on the fact that Colonel Ramon's parents were both Holocaust survivors and that Ramon took aboard with him Holocaust-related items and literature.

Others point to the U.S. government and believe it is a self-inflicted disaster, a "textbook psychological warfare operation" designed to create public anger against Iraq and the wider Arab world to prepare people psychologically to support the Iraq War. Even without explicit confirmation from the government, the tacit link would be enough to increase support for a controversial conflict. A similar plan to this, entitled the "Northwoods" plan, was developed in the 1960s. It was drawn up by the Joint Chiefs of Staff and aimed to blame Cuba if anything went wrong during the mission to launch John Glenn as the first American to orbit the Earth in 1962.

Apocryphal stories also emerged suggesting Colonel Ramon was conducting secret experiments on the shuttle mission on behalf of Israel's Institute of Biological Research, looking at ways of combating Saddam Hussein's potential weapons of mass destruction threat. It was alleged Ramon was using covert cameras to survey desert dust and wind-drifts emanating from Iraq's deserts, providing intelligence that would assist in repelling possible future attacks; but the likelihood of this seems remote.

# Spam

This theory follows that the government has conspired against the free-will choices of the people in producing this processed food substance. The truth regarding Spam is that it plays an important role in the conspiracy to sell humans to aliens in exchange for some relatively unimportant laser weapons and mind-control technology. The agreement stated that when they abducted our citizens, officials would turn a blind eye and in return they would provide us with the bargained-for technology.

In reality it wasn't such a bad deal. All we had to do was allow the aliens to implant mind-control devices into approximately one in forty of our blissfully unaware citizens. All victims would be returned to where they came from and have no conscious memory of the horrendous ordeal. Unless they took the conscious step of hypnosis they would never actually know what had hit them.

So where does Spam come into it all? Because of an undeveloped digestive system, the aliens cannot eat food in the same manner as we do. They remove intestinal and hormonal extracts from us and cook them, and then dip their body parts in the stew, hoping that some of the nutritional substance will seep through their skin. But here's the catch. Humans who have not been subjected to carefully measured doses of Spam just don't taste as good. It's a simple equation. No Spam equals no abduction.

This is, in fact, the purpose of the alien's "anal probe," which is used to extract fecal matter from the lower intestine to see if the human meal has been sufficiently spiced with enough Spam. If there is enough taste, the human is cut up and placed into one of their feeding vats. If not, he or she is implanted with an electronic device, which causes the victim to crave more Spam.

One begins to see why the government has gone to such great lengths to keep the distasteful truth from us. And what is more, one starts to appreciate why there is such a strong intergalactic drive to force us to produce more and more Spam. And one can ask why the producers of Spam food products have recently launched such an extensive marketing campaign.

# Sphinx and the
# Great Pyramids

The ancient Egyptians built their monuments on a scale that continues to impress even modern scholars and tourists. The grandest of their monuments, and possibly the most debated, are the Great Pyramids at Giza. These structures, built wholly of solid stone blocks weighing two hundred tons each, have fascinated visitors since their construction, the techniques of which have been lost to history.

Recent evidence suggests that the Egyptian Pharaohs, scheming to create a lasting and powerful display of Egyptian ingenuity, created the structures for the express purpose of confusing future civilizations as to just exactly how they were built. With theories of vast slave pools, unknown ancient technology and even alien assistance, the mystery of Egypt and the mystery of the pyramids will likely live on far into human history. However, startling new evidence has suggested that perhaps the monuments were not built by the Egyptians at all.

The Great Sphinx of Giza is one of the world's oldest mysteries. It is probably the greatest relic of a distant past, but one that asks more questions than it answers and one that could potentially reveal information that could throw new light on our entire civilization.

The Sphinx is not built out of quarried rock like the pyramids and temples that it guards, but rather out of the unbroken foundation. It has a man's (or arguably a woman's) head and the body of a lion. It is 66 feet high, 240 feet long and has the most extraordinary expression looking out of this world into infinity. Most Egyptologists, and most Egyptians for that matter, believe that the Sphinx was built in around 2500 B.C. in the time of the pharaoh Chephren (or Khafre), who is identified with the Second Pyramid at Giza. Yet recent research has shown that this theory is little more than legend, but a theory that is well worth upholding on the Egyptians' part, for the monumental edifice has become a symbol of their kingdom.

John A. West had visited the statue many times, and it had always seemed to him to be something apart, something far older than known civilization. Reading a book on Egypt by the French author and mathematician Schwaller de Lubicz, he came across the theory that there were signs of water erosion on the body of the Sphinx. West realized that the weathering patterns on the Sphinx were not horizontal as seen on other monuments at Giza, but vertical. Horizontal weathering is the result of prolonged exposure to strong winds and sandstorms. There have been plenty of these in the arid area of the Sahara, but could water have caused the vertical weathering on the Sphinx? Water from where?

In 1991 Dr. Robert Schoch, a prominent geologist and professor from Boston University, examined the weathering on the Sphinx and concluded that the patterns must have been caused by torrential rain, concluding that the Sphinx must have been built in an era when such rains were common in this area, and that the other monuments must have come many years later. This would suggest that the Sphinx was built before the most ancient of Egyptians, before the very first dynasties thousands of years before

Christ, before, in fact, recorded history. And this unravels quite staggering possibilities.

The Sphinx is quite possibly the most remarkable monument in the world. It is quite unlike anything either the ancient Egyptians or even our modern culture could build. It seems to belong to an ancient culture, and one which must have had far greater knowledge than ours. Its face is surprisingly modern and its expression is one of such wisdom and profundity that it suggests a knowledge far beyond our puny mortal efforts. We can only surmise at what secret the Sphinx guards, but whatever it is, the Egyptians do not want it revealed.

The pharaonic head of the Sphinx is out of proportion with the body. Could it have originally been a leonine head, carved twelve thousand years ago to mark the Age of Leo, which was then rediscovered just four thousand years ago by the Egyptians and recarved at that point in honor of their pharaoh?

A series of surveys have also indicated the existence of several tunnels under the Great Sphinx itself, leading to an unexplored chamber about twenty-five feet beneath the great paws of the statue. We can only surmise as to what the contents of this chamber might be, but the possibilities are endless. The remnants of an ancient civilization could be stored here. And if this ancient civilization was capable of building the Sphinx, revelation of its other capabilities could be extremely enlightening. Perhaps therein lies the riddle of the Sphinx.

Moreover, in March 1993 a small door was discovered at the end of a long narrow shaft in the Great Pyramid. Since then, the principal researcher, German Rudolph Gantenbrink, has been forbidden from continuing the exploration. The Egyptian Antiquities Authorities gave the excuse that, in leaking the news to the British press, Gantenbrink broke a rule of archaeology. Egyptian authorities were adamant that the find was of no importance. It would seem that the authorities were attempting to hide something.

# Squirrels

The squirrel has a brain the size of an oversized pea. But research has shown that it demonstrates a quite extraordinary intelligence and memory capacity that may be endangering the future of mankind. It is all too easy to underestimate the capabilities of these animals. But we are facing the prospect of world domination if we do not become aware of the potential dangers confronting us.

Every year, a squirrel will store away about ten thousand nuts, and their very survival depends on their ability to find where they have hidden them. Their memory capacity is enormous, hiding each nut in a different place and then being able to find it again. A series of experiments in California attempted to research something of this intelligence. The first experiment placed a nut in the same position over a number of days, testing the squirrel's spatial memory. The second experiment, however, was more complicated, changing the route to the nut so that the squirrel had alternative routes. And the squirrels demonstrated that they were not relying on merely retracing their steps. When the route was changed, they could still find the nut at the end of it.

However, what is disturbing is that there would appear to be suspicious squirrel activities taking place in Europe. Squirrels seem to be behind much of society's ills, controlling governments and eliminating anyone who stands in their path. Most frightening of all, while the prospect of a squirrel takeover is scary enough, it has been suggested that stoats, ferrets and hamsters may also be involved. Their role is as yet undefined, but the possibility of major military attack cannot be ruled out.

While the whereabouts of the headquarters is unknown, possibilities have been narrowed down to one of the following areas: Red Square, Moscow; under the Eiffel Tower, Paris; in a Romanian sewer; Stoke-on-Trent, England. One can only live in hope that the true whereabouts will be discovered in the not too distant future.

As a warning: Offering squirrels food may lull them into a false sense of security, but it would seem that they are starting to see through this bluff and may attack viciously. It is not worth making oneself known personally to them. There comes a time in every civilization when humankind must unite and fight for the common good. It is to be sincerely hoped that this way we can prevent rodent domination.

# Stalin

Joseph Stalin's "friend" and political aide and confidant, Sergei Kirov, had become a potential rival for Communist Party leadership. He thus had to be removed from the political scene. Stalin arranged for Kirov's murder and placed the blame on the Zinoviev faction. Stalin was a cunning conspirator and foresaw the wave of official adulation for Kirov. Robert Tucker writes in *Stalin in Power* that "The instant Kirov cult was blended into the Stalin cult, which took on an added lustre, Kirov became 'Comrade Stalin's best comrade-in-arms and friend.' Stalin was shown in the honor guard with Kirov in old photos and as the first mourner at the Red Square funeral."

But this single murder was part of a much larger conspiracy whose aims were far broader than the removal of a single political competitor. Tucker writes: "For the conspirator from above, the prime purpose of Kirov's murder was to make possible an official finding that Soviet Russia was beset by a conspiracy that had done away with Kirov as part of a much larger plan of terrorist action against the regime." In this way, Stalin had the excuse to begin the Great Purge, which claimed millions of innocent lives.

Even before the murder, Stalin had decreed a statute allowing the newly created Special Board to have the final word on "persons deemed socially dangerous." This allowed for the loosest of interpretations of "socially dangerous," which could be taken as anything that went against the will of Stalin. Just as Hitler was quite prepared to persuade the public that his mass genocide was for their own good, so Stalin had no qualms in making out that his program was one of social awareness and justice.

# Stargate

The civilization of ancient Egypt has provided interest and intrigue across the world for centuries, but it has also generated enormous fascination with conspiracy theorists. The Pyramids and the Sphinx are such compelling structures that it seems remarkable they could have been conceived and built by a culture thousands of years ago.

Many books have been written about the origins of these structures in recent years, some involving extraterrestrials and visitors from other dimensions. Popular theories suggest that the Egyptian civilization was created or assisted by superior technology from outer space. But one of the most interesting theories currently put forward contradicts all of these and believes the explanation is to be found here on Earth. *The Stargate Conspiracy* by Lynn Picknett and Clive Prince claims that conspiracy theories about a mythical Stargate are all part of a greater but less documented conspiracy themselves. The bogus idea of extraterrestrial intervention is a deliberate red herring on the part of a much wider conspiracy involving intelligence agencies, whose aim is that people will feel they are subordinate to some form of superior extraterrestrial race. This would create a dependency among humanity upon outside forces and an inferiority complex across the human race. Messages then "intercepted" by governments and intelligence agencies could be used to manipulate a country's population under the guise of extraterrestrial orders, and create authoritarian, fascist dictatorships.

Which authors are involved in promulgating this idea is not entirely clear, but as these beliefs have reached the public domain, those with fanciful minds have unwittingly helped to spread the idea further, lending it unwarranted credibility.

These ideas are not new. In his book *The Controllers: A New Hypothesis of Alien Abduction,* Martin Cannon discusses his belief that reported alien abductions are in fact planned kidnappings by the security services, including MI6, the CIA and the National Security Agency in the United States. These people are then used for experiments in mind control and other clandestine technologies. When these incidents of abduction are reported they are never taken seriously by the mainstream media. Those making the claims are simply brushed aside or considered lunatics.

There is a long history of the intelligence services and the military divulging false information concerning extraterrestrials to preserve the fascination for aliens among the general public. Anonymous tip-offs concerning the activities at Area 51 have been given to journalists to create a fabricated frenzy. It always suits agencies like the CIA to create a culture of dependency among citizens, enabling the government to press ahead with its own autocratic agenda unhindered.

It could be that much of the material on alien conspiracies is generated not by well-intentioned authors and researchers but by secret intelligence operatives and government-sponsored writers to create widely held myths that divert attention from the real truth that needs to be uncovered. The world's fascination with ancient Egypt could be the greatest example of this grand scheme.

# Subliminal Advertising

Subliminal advertising is a topic of continual controversy among academics, the advertising industry and
big business in general, with the public left in the middle
not knowing whom to believe or whom to trust. Arguments
and insults have been traded between scholars and advertisers repeatedly with both sides claiming to speak the truth
and accusing the other of casting damaging aspersions.

Whenever conspiracy theories are discussed they are
often linked to political events, whether by partisan trou-
blemakers or well-intentioned truth-seekers. George W.
Bush and his party were accused of using subliminal messages during his 2000 election campaign in Florida. In a
Republican ad criticizing Democratic candidate Al Gore's
prescription drug proposal the word "rats" appears briefly
on screen over the words "The Gore Prescription Plan."
The letters then form part of the next message, which is
"Bureaucrats decide."

Owing to the extremely fractious nature of the 2000
election race, and the events in Florida especially, accusing
fingers were pointed towards the Bush campaign team. Al
Gore claimed, "I've never seen anything like it. I think it

speaks for itself." When he was asked who he thought was behind the "rats" message he stated, "That's obvious." The ad was shown 4,400 times in thirty-three television markets across America.

The topic of subliminal advertising is a contentious one. Arguments rage among academics about whether it even exists. Subliminal messages often focus on society's taboos. According to Dr. Wilson Bryan Key, topics such as sex, death, incest, homosexuality and pagan symbols are all used by advertising companies to get a secret message into a viewer's mind without them realizing it consciously. The advertising agencies claim that any hidden symbols are pure coincidence, by mistake, or the result of individual artists going beyond their remit. In his research, however, Key says advertising agencies spend thousands of dollars and hundreds of design hours making sure their ads are pitched perfectly to their intended target, right down to using death symbols, screaming faces, images of animals and of sexual gratification.

With no laws to prevent this kind of activity, there is little to stop advertising agencies resorting to the use of subliminal messages. It is very disturbing indeed to consider the power advertisers have to conspire to change society's behavior in ways we wouldn't even be aware of.

# Television

Once World War II was over, mass media and entertainment changed forever. No longer were people having to rely on crackly wirelesses and slide projectors focused onto an old sheet. This new device called television worked very much like radio and transformed broadcast waves into sound, accompanied by moving pictures. No longer were the audiences forced to rely on their own imaginations and suspend all pretense at reality because finally images were portrayed in realistic detail. No one can deny that it has certainly proved to be a popular and enduring pastime.

But behind the development and marketing of television lay a worldwide conspiracy put into motion by the United States government and the newly formed CIA. They realized that television would completely revolutionize mass entertainment. The CIA made development and marketing an absolute priority. By the time the television came onto the market, a whole range of entertainment specials had been created.

The appeal of television to the government was all too simple. If the vast majority of the public were occupied, attention would be drawn away from secret defense programs. It was hoped that with this modern distraction agent, the United States could use what strategies they saw fit in competing with the Soviet Union during the Cold War.

# *Titanic*

In 1912 the English cruise liner *Titanic* sank to the bottom of the North Atlantic, taking some two-thirds of its passengers to their icy deaths. The tragedy of the largest liner of its time has long been attributed to collision with an iceberg by those on board both the ship itself and the rescue vessels.

The ship lay undiscovered for over seventy years until Dr. Robert Ballard of the Woods Hale Oceanographic Institute led an expedition that successfully located the sunken shell. Subsequent trips to the wreckage more thoroughly examined the shattered hull and new evidence brought about a startling new conclusion. Forget the iceberg. The *Titanic* had been attacked by torpedo.

By 1912 the Germans had perfected the U-Boat and built several prototypes for testing. The German government distrusted the English, and set to prove them wrong when they proclaimed the ship "unsinkable." The U-Boat glided quietly out into the North Atlantic and crept up on the luxury liner. It was simply good fortune and coincidence that the ship happened to pass next to an iceberg; realizing that this would mask their action, the Germans torpedoed the same side of the ship. The resulting damage sunk the *Titanic* and its passengers. The German U-Boat slipped silently away and let the iceberg have the glory.

# Trailer Parks

On October 29, 1929, the worst stock market crash in the nation's history occurred in the United States. Suddenly the nation plunged from being a fast growing economic power into a deep and long-lasting crisis of financial loss and chronic unemployment. In 1932 Franklin Roosevelt won over Herbert Hoover in the presidential elections and embarked on the huge social reform intended to repair the nation. His program ranged from funding for public services to instituting social welfare. The nation's predicament slowly improved and Roosevelt was reelected in 1936, 1940 and 1944. This extensive economic reform, however, had its darker side.

Roosevelt knew that part of the nation's problem was simply that it was overpopulated, but at the same time, realized that a Hitleresque genocide by the military may have solved the population crisis, but that it would not do the country's reputation much good. So as an alternative he hit upon a plan to remove large segments of the country's population without losing face.

Roosevelt secretly contacted various architects and engineers and instructed them to make as a priority the design of a mobile house, or "trailer home." These would offer low-income families a home, relative comfort and community life. Land was bought in the midwestern states and a series of trailer parks was created.

However, the plan involved making the location of the trailer parks the region where more tornadoes occur than the total amount in the rest of the world. Thus, the plan went, multitudes of tornadoes would hit the trailer parks, eliminating whole families in natural disasters for which no individual could be held responsible. And every year, hundreds are injured when tornadoes tear paths of destruction through trailer parks, just as Roosevelt intended.

# Tupac Shakur

The uncontested facts: After leaving the Mike Tyson fight in Las Vegas on Saturday, September 7, 1996, Tupac Shakur was shot five times from a car that pulled up close to his. He initially survived the shooting and was taken to a nearby hospital. He was pronounced dead on September 13, 1996. That was a Friday the thirteenth.

There have been plenty of conspiracy theories around the murder, but none has caught on like the notion that Shakur's death is all one big hoax. The theory holds that Shakur wanted to be free of the stifling publicity that went along with his high-profile outlaw lifestyle and that he's now living it up on a desert island somewhere.

Some of the clues include:

• He is seen crucified on the cover of one of his CDs, which would suggest that he will rise again.

• A music video released conveniently just days after his death shows Tupac being murdered, presumably to convince the public that this was what really did happen.

• Tupac always wore a bulletproof vest, no matter where he went. Why didn't he wear it to a very public event like a Tyson fight? Some believe he wanted to make it plausible that a shot would kill him.

• In most of his songs, he talks about being buried, so why was he allegedly cremated the day after he died? Furthermore, it is highly unconventional to cremate someone the day after death without a full investigation. In fact, it is illegal to bury someone who has been murdered without a postmortem.

• Why couldn't the police locate the white car from which the bullets were fired? After all, Las Vegas is in the middle of the desert, and it would seem really quite improbable that it escaped without being witnessed.

• Tupac's entourage was notorious for having a gangsterlike image. So why did none of them shoot back?

# Turin Shroud 1

The public exhibition of one of the most disputed relics in history has been the subject of much controversy. We know that the large sheet bearing the imprint of a man is at least several hundred years old and may be as old as two thousand. The bearded, long-haired man in the image would seem to have suffered wounds associated with crucifixion and certainly suggests relation to Jesus' body. It bears marks along the forehead, which one could presume came from the crown of thorns, flogging wounds and even a cut to the right of his chest. The cloth would appear to be stained with ancient blood stains.

What rouses the experts' suspicion is how the imprint of the man ever found its way onto the cloth in the first place. It gives an impression similar to a photographic negative, but that would have been quite an achievement two thousand years ago. Or even one thousand years ago for that matter. One theory goes that Leonardo da Vinci had the technological knowledge to create a photographic image, and that in fact the image of the shroud is a photographic self-portrait of Leonardo himself.

One scientist put forward the theory that the imprint on

the shroud is in fact a painting, claiming to find traces of paint on the cloth. However, arguments against this would say that the paint could have rubbed off the paintings that the shroud covered in attempts to sanctify them. And others have dismissed the theory by claiming not to have found paintbrush strokes on the shroud.

One piece of evidence pointing to a forgery is that the nail wounds are in the palms of the hands, as was traditionally believed to be the case with Jesus. Historical evidence of crucifixions points to this being a physical impossibility, however: a nail through the palm could not support the body's weight—it would tear through the bones and muscles. Crucifixion was only possible by placing the nail through the wrist, which had a strong enough bone structure. If Jesus' shroud is a fabrication, then it followed tradition rather than scientific fact.

While it may be a clever fake, the origins of the shroud are ambiguous. Because even if it had been fabricated in the Middle Ages as the ultimate relic, the precision of the image is astounding. And this cannot explain away the blood stains. One theory would have it that the shroud is not only what it claims to be but that it is more than this in being none other than The Holy Grail of myth. Another theorist puts forward the view that the imprint of the man is not actually Jesus but one of the Knights Templar, one of the legendary guardians of the Grail.

# Turin Shroud 2

The Turin Shroud has, for the third time since its relocation to Turin, nearly been the victim of fire. Early on April 14, 1997, firemen arrived at the scene to find flames and smoke pouring out of the tops of the cathedral and the Guarini Chapel, which was built to house the shroud. Local fireman and hero Mario Trematore used a sledgehammer to break the bulletproof glass that protected the relic, and then carried it to safety.

The shroud escaped damage, but the Renaissance cathedral and the chapel, designed by architect Guarino Guarini, suffered extensive damage. The official report points to an electrical failure as the source of the fire, but an unofficial source has revealed an anti-Catholic conspiracy that targeted the shroud. It is alleged that members of the Southern Baptist Church of North America and extremist fundamentalist factions of the Protestant church may have set fire to the chapel to destroy the shroud. This would coincide with a new period of attack against Roman Catholicism by reactionary Protestant forces. The destruction of the shroud would certainly have provoked widespread disruption and trauma in the Roman Catholic Church worldwide. The ensuing havoc would have provided rival factions with the perfect opportunity to launch an attack.

The Baptist Church has officially rejected the shroud as a fraud, quoting recent scientific work aimed at dating the linen. However, although the studies indicate that the shroud may originate in the Middle Ages, they cannot reach any precise date of origin, nor explain the image for which the shroud is so famous. Since the fire, the shroud has been moved to a secret monastery for safekeeping.

# Virtual Conspiracy

There seems to be little doubt that there must have been a conspiracy to bring Bill Clinton down during his presidency. But this was no ordinary conspiracy. Unlike the conspirators that met in boarding houses to plot Abraham Lincoln's assassination, this was something of a completely different order, a "virtual" conspiracy.

In a traditional conspiracy, individuals all come together and when they finally move, speed is vitally important. Secrecy is essential. A virtual conspiracy has the same objective of bringing a leader down, but the tactics are different. It starts in the open and requires publicity to grow and gain supporters. By making their moves overtly, they attract others to their cause and to one another.

Freedom of expression is the name of the game here and the virtual conspirators channel charges and make false allegations through the press. Whether the allegations succeed or fail, they invariably have some effect, making the target more and more vulnerable.

In this way, the virtual conspirators weren't concerned with whether the Clintons did or didn't murder Vincent Foster, as was alleged, nor whether the evidence pointed towards Foster having committed suicide or not. The objective was to get the media to voice the idea of the Clintons as murderers in the hope that someone would come forward with proof. Similarly, it was of little consequence to them whether the Clinton administration did or didn't allocate grave sites at Arlington National Cemetery for political supporters. And the details of his various sexual adventures were of no interest whatsoever. Whether Clinton raped a woman in Arkansas when he was Attorney General in his home state was neither here nor there. What was important to these virtual conspirators was that these provocative questions wormed their way into the press.

And the fantastic thing about being a virtual conspirator is that you can spread the most outrageous rumors about who you want and not get personally accused. The reporter you conned may not be best pleased, but the more scandalous the story the better it will sell. An angry denial from the president himself generates yet more coverage of the actual charge. It would seem that if they were unable to defeat him at the elections, the best way for Clinton's enemies (or those of any other major political leader) to have brought him down was by virtual conspiracy.

# Waco

American officials are delving into the evidence of what really happened at Waco, pressing for the truth into what the government really did in the disastrous 1993 raid. Steve Stockman, a Texan, wrote an article putting forward the conspiracy theory that the Clinton authorities stormed the community in an effort to gain support for gun control.

It cannot be denied that the FBI and ATF did indeed storm into the apocalyptic religious sect. And even if they were not part of some gun-control conspiracy as Stockman would have it, they did provoke the hostile response of David Koresh and his followers and were in large part responsible for the blazing inferno. According to Peter Boyer, who wrote an enlightening analysis of the unfortunate ATF raid and the disastrous FBI assault, FBI officials played on the ignorance of the newly appointed Attorney General Janet Reno, who simply did not know enough about the situation, by failing to inform her of vital plans and information. By claiming that Koresh was carrying out acts of child abuse inside the compound, the FBI virtually forced Reno into ordering a paramilitary attack on the compound. Whether child abuse did or did not take place we don't know. But we do know that the results of the assault were disastrous.

So what really did happen at Waco? Several years after the tragedy, the best evidence still seems to suggest that Reno was tyrannized by the FBI. It was the FBI who pushed for the raid in the first place. And it is Republicans who continue to gain on the political front.

# Who Will Take Over
the World?

Once upon a time, the Soviet Union seemed poised to steamroll Europe. It was blatantly obvious who was behind all our political, economic and personal troubles. The Communists were convenient scapegoats for everything. All they needed to do was to march in and take over without firing a shot.

But as the new millennium approached, a strange phenomenon took place. The USSR collapsed and split up. Looking back, the West began to wonder how on earth they could ever have been anxious about the Russians in the first place. The nation of Aeroflot, a nation which, to an outsider, seemed to pride themselves as much on their vodka consumption as on a stable market economy, seemed to pose little threat for world domination. And just to put the icing on the cake, both Britain and the U.S. had shown their true colors during the Gulf War and had proven that, if necessary, they could get together a million-strong army in a matter of days.

After the fall of the USSR, conspiracy theorists had to revise their world view somewhat. Of course, the whole thing could have been just a crafty Soviet plot, but the odd skeptic began to ask who was most likely to dominate the world. Once things are conveniently out of control, a State of Emergency will be declared and all hell will break loose. The following are the three main threats:

**1. Alien Nation.** A supersecret government within the American government called MJ-12 has apparently been presiding over the "alien question" since the days of President Dwight D. Eisenhower. MJ-12 has been keeping all sorts of information from us, including alien abductions, cattle mutilations and crashed saucers. If that wasn't bad enough, a whole host of secret deals were cast with one or more alien races. The theory goes that rapid technological advancements since the 1950s came not from the billions of dollars spent on scientific research but from donated technology from spacemen. Some would have it that cattle mutilations and assaults are in fact a manifestation of a long-term experiment to turn humans into cattle to act as a host for genetically manufactured aliens. Moreover, William Cooper, an alleged former intelligence officer in the U.S. government, has claimed that if the secret should get out, MJ-12 has a plan to round up all sorts of people and send them off to concentration camps. Apparently this was the real reason behind the JFK assassination, as Kennedy had apparently known about the conspiracy and was about to make an announcement to the nation.

**2. Illuminati.** The whole institution of the Illuminati is surrounded in mystery, not least of all because no one really knows what it is made up of. We do know that there are many different Illuminati groups, all with different kinds of secret knowledge, which take over all kinds of organizations ranging from top chain supermarkets to radio and television broadcasting agencies to Mrs. Boggins' tea shop round the corner. For the last several hundred years, they have been condemned by governments and religions as being linked to conspiracies for a one-world government.

The plan for worldwide control was formulated over two hundred years ago by a group of leading European bankers made up of a dozen or so rich families, led by money lenders and industrialists. It was initiated in Bavaria by a professor named Adam Weishaupt. His theories revolved around the ideal of utopic democracy which, he felt, could only be achieved by means of a one-world government. The conspiracy has infiltrated much of the history of the Western world, and includes the Bilderbergers, the Club of Rome, the Council on Foreign Relations and the Trilateral Commission. The Illuminati have always been closely linked to the Freemasons and, indeed, the start of the cult involved domination of the upper ranks of Continental Freemasonry.

The Illuminati still attempt to recruit students with exceptional mental ability coming from affluent backgrounds. They then convince them that men of above-average intelligence have the right to rule the world simply because the masses do not know what is good for them, physically, economically or spiritually. Their aims, however, are no longer quite so philanthropic.

Mrs. Boggins' tea shop down the road may look innocuous enough, but remember that she could be one of THEM. Their superior technological knowhow means that they have more than enough expertise to carry out their projects for absolute domination. Their primary aims are the complete extinction of independence and the establishment of mindless obedience to the party line. To keep themselves amused, they commit petty crimes (just think what could have gone into Mrs. Boggins' tea which she sets before you) to cause as much confusion as possible.

Their plan is for a one-world government to be made up of a key dictator with his government of a few billionaires, Communists and scientists who have shown loyalty to the cause. The rest of us are to be completely enslaved to this elite.

**3. Saddam Hussein.** Saddam Hussein has been quite possibly the most dangerous threat to the planet's stability and safety since Hitler. Allied bombings of Baghdad were not enough to silence him and conflict continued, eventually culminating in a second war in the Gulf.

It was clear that this tyrannical leader, who has imposed a reign of terror on his subjects and has been an ongoing threat to the rest of the world, needed to be stopped. Rumors of conspiracy plots have been in the air ever since the troubles began, and, it is hinted, weapons have been developed and perfected so that a single shot can now be fired accurately from several miles away.

But Saddam—who was supposedly captured in December 2003—is no fool. He is quite aware that he is unpopular, and he has always been aware of the threat to his personal safety. So he would go nowhere without a bodyguard. He had servants to taste his food. He mastered the art of self-defense in all walks of life; and this includes having a series of doubles. Some might even call them clones.

Saddam's clones serve their purpose, and the implications of having them are potentially quite enormous. The obvious question is: Is it really Saddam Hussein being held in coalition custody? If Saddam Hussein is actually a committee, it is of little consequence whether the original one is captured or free, alive or dead.

# Whore of Babylon

Ancient Mesopotamia, the birthplace of civilization, owned several cities which would play a significant role in Western culture. Babylon developed into one of these cities, reaching its economic and cultural peak under Nebuchadnezzar, the famous conqueror of Judea in the Bible. Early in its history, however, Babylon was but one of a multitude of small towns whose very upkeep was threatened by constant invasions.

Well aware of their situation, the leaders of the city came up with a brilliant idea to elevate Babylon to power. Realizing that sex would probably attract and sell better and faster than any politics or religion, and probably on a much more long-term basis, they established the legend of the Whore of Babylon, a mythical figure who would come to represent the royally encouraged enterprise of prostitution.

Babylon's king and leaders actively encouraged the spread of myths telling of orgies and debauchery on a mammoth level. Soon, Babylon's reputation as a city of pleasure spread far and wide as men seeking instant gratification and fulfillment came to the city in hordes, which subsequently resulted in increased tourism and commerce.

This newly discovered wealth enabled the city to grow and prosper. Even as late as the fourth century B.C., Alexander the Great, attracted to the temptations of the city, camped his army within the walls of Babylon to spend the winter. Only during the first centuries A.D. did the idea of the Whore of Babylon as something sinful take over from the representation of prosperity and opulence.

# Zebras

Few of us know the web of conspiracy surrounding renowned Zachariah the Zebra at a well-known zoo. The fate of the poor aforementioned animal seemed to be set in stone when he finally passed away after years of faithful service to the zoo. Distress failed to describe the emotions of the children who had traveled from all corners of the country to see poor old Zack.

And so, decided the authorities, action had to be taken. The expressions on the faces of the hordes of distraught children who had rushed so expectantly to Zack's cage was just too much to bear. An artful disguise was undertaken. A horse was imported from the adjoining cage and was painted black and white. And no one noticed. The delight of the children knew no bounds. Zack was back.

This project was not without its complications, however—not least of all that Zack had to be repainted every week, and every two hours if it rained. But this seems of little consequence, seeing as rumor was threatening closure of the zoo. And if it took standing in the rain painting a horse black and white to avoid redundancy, the zoo workers were quite happy to undertake the task.